Susan, Duchess of Hamilton *by Willes Maddox*

THE ART OF JEWELLERY IN SCOTLAND

EDITED BY

ROSALIND K MARSHALL AND GEORGE R DALGLEISH

WITH CONTRIBUTIONS BY
CHARLOTTE GERE   ELIZABETH GORING   DIANA SCARISBRICK

SCOTTISH NATIONAL PORTRAIT GALLERY
EDINBURGH   HMSO

Designed by Graham Galloway
HMSO Graphic Design Edinburgh

HMSO publications are available from:

HMSO Bookshops

71 Lothian Road, Edinburgh EH 9AZ   031-228 4181
49 High Holborn, London WC1V 6HB 071-873 0011
(Counter service only)
258 Broad Street, Birmingham B1 2HE 021-643 3740
Southey House, 33 Wine Street, Bristol BS1 2BQ
(0272) 264306
9-21 Princess Street, Manchester M60 8AS   061-834 7201
80 Chichester Street, Belfast BT1 4JY   (0232) 238451

HMSO Publications Centre

(Mail and telephone orders only)
PO Box 276, London SW8 5DT
Telephone orders 071-873 9090
General enquiries 071-873 0011
(queuing system in operation for both numbers)

HMSO's Accreditied Agents

(see Yellow Pages)

And through good booksellers

ISBN 0 11 494154 8

CONTENTS

FOREWORD *7*

JEWELLERY AND PORTRAITS *8*

I THE SIXTEENTH CENTURY *12*

II THE SEVENTEENTH AND EIGHTEENTH CENTURIES *24*

III COMMEMORATIVE AND MEMORIAL JEWELLERY *44*

IV HIGHLAND JEWELLERY *56*

V THE NINETEENTH CENTURY *66*

VI THE TWENTIETH CENTURY *77*

FURTHER READING *94*

This book breaks new ground, tracing the history of jewellery in Scotland from the sixteenth century to the present day, both by means of the jewels themselves and the evidence that can be gathered from portraits about how they were worn. The idea for such a survey was first conceived by the Edinburgh jewellers Hamilton & Inches and we are happy to mark the 125th anniversary of this important Scottish company by means of the exhibition they are sponsoring at the Scottish National Portrait Gallery and which has been mounted in conjunction with this publication.

Many people, too many to mention here, have contributed to the realisation of both the book and the exhibition. We are particularly grateful to those owners of jewellery and paintings who have lent items to the exhibition and allowed us to reproduce them here.

Particular mention must, however, be made of the Director and Trustees of the National Museums of Scotland who have lent massively to the exhibition and whose curators, George Dalgleish and Elizabeth Goring, have been enabled to work on the project with Rosalind Marshall of the Portrait Gallery who has guided the entire work. Thanks are also due to the jewellery historians, Charlotte Gere and Diana Scarisbrick, for their contributions. Finally, Alison Boocock must be thanked for producing the typescript of this book with both accuracy and speed.

Timothy Clifford
Director of the National
Galleries of Scotland

Duncan Thomson
Keeper of the Scottish
National Portrait Gallery

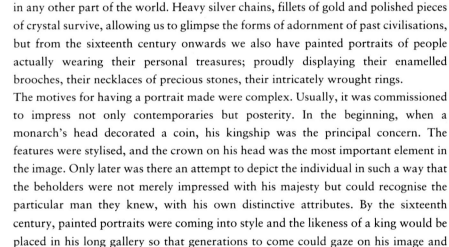

JEWELLERY AND PORTRAITS

detail of 14 Lady Rothes and daughters

From earliest times, men and women have worn jewellery as an expression of status, sentiment or even superstition, and this is as true in Scotland as in any other part of the world. Heavy silver chains, fillets of gold and polished pieces of crystal survive, allowing us to glimpse the forms of adornment of past civilisations, but from the sixteenth century onwards we also have painted portraits of people actually wearing their personal treasures; proudly displaying their enamelled brooches, their necklaces of precious stones, their intricately wrought rings.

The motives for having a portrait made were complex. Usually, it was commissioned to impress not only contemporaries but posterity. In the beginning, when a monarch's head decorated a coin, his kingship was the principal concern. The features were stylised, and the crown on his head was the most important element in the image. Only later was there an attempt to depict the individual in such a way that the beholders were not merely impressed with his majesty but could recognise the particular man they knew, with his own distinctive attributes. By the sixteenth century, painted portraits were coming into style and the likeness of a king would be placed in his long gallery so that generations to come could gaze on his image and reflect upon his power.

The delineation of status remained a vital part of portraiture long after the early period. Not only monarchs but the aristocracy and the striving middle class wished to be represented in such a way that their riches and their importance were clearly evident. Visual indications of a man's place in society were vital and so the king had his ermine, the academic wore a scholar's gown, the widow was draped in black, and the noble was arrayed not only in velvets and furs but in the gold chains and buttons and rings which were direct and unambiguous statements of his wealth.

At this time, artists painted with an eye for accuracy and for the most minute detail, and there is little doubt that the jewellery we see in their pictures really did exist. They do not seem to have invented accessories and it has been possible for costume and jewellery historians to match up, for example, the garments and the gems noted in Queen Elizabeth I of England's inventories with the finery which appears in her many pictures. It is only very rarely that the actual jewels shown in portraits still exist: throughout the centuries owners have had their jewellery broken up so that the gems could be re-set in more modern style. However, the miniature case which adorns Lady Anne Livingston's bodice (10) has been identified as the one preserved to this day in the Fitzwilliam Museum (11).

The need for accuracy extended into the early seventeenth century, but after that considerations of taste became more important. It was no longer considered fitting to load one's person with jewels and precious stones. Henceforth, masculine jewellery took the form of a signet ring, a fine watch, a discreet pair of cuff-links or an unobtrusive tie-pin. There were other ways of demonstrating wealth, and men took to emphasising their riches, their culture and their ancient lineage by building fine houses, laying out gardens and by emblazoning their coats of arms in stone, on silver, on the doors of their coaches, on their books and on their soup plates.

Some of the Scottish peerage collected paintings: Old Masters from Italy and the Low Countries. Almost all of them commissioned family portraits, and by now they were anxious that their features should be represented in a lifelike way. They might don the garb of Ancient Romans, in a vain endeavour to achieve an air of timeless dignity, but they still wanted to look like themselves. They had no intention of acquiring a painting of a handsome stranger. As a result, the studios of dead artists were usually stacked with canvases, some unfinished, others completed but never collected by the person who had commissioned them, for the simple reason that they did not resemble the sitter.

Men cared about likeness, and women were even more anxious to achieve a recognisable representation of themselves. For them, the principal motive was not the desire to impress but the need to have a reminder of absent friends. Propelled into arranged marriages by their parents and sent to far-off parts of the country with little-known husbands, these young women sought and treasured pictures of the mothers, sisters and friends they now so rarely saw and their correspondence often shows them seeking copies of existing pictures: 'dark shadows of my friends and kindred about me', as Anne, Countess of Balcarres put it in 1651, 'if so be thereby I may deceive my solitud'. In such circumstances it would have been considered vulgar to present oneself weighed down with enamelled gold and gems. A single string of pearls and a pair of pendant pearl earrings were considered the only adornments necessary for a high-born lady.

Now it might be supposed that theological considerations played their part in this shift in taste. From the late 1630s onwards many of the wives of the Scottish nobility were strict Presbyterians with Covenanting sympathies. For the husbands, in attendance at court, forever vying with their rivals, status was all-important and while they wrote and spoke disapprovingly of the vanity of the world and the need to disassociate themselves from the frivolities of a corrupt society, in practice they were as attached to pomp and magnificence and outward show as any of their ancestors ever had been.

Similarly, although their wives were able to stay privately at home and rarely ventured to the dissolute capital, they too knew that it was necessary to maintain their rank by appearing in rich fabrics. It would be a mistake, however, to imagine that there was some form of puritanical dress favoured by these ladies. On the

detail of 10 Lady Anne Livingston

detail of 12 Lady Napier

9

contrary, there is no difference whatsoever to be discerned between the clothing and the jewellery worn by a Presbyterian, an Episcopalian or a Roman Catholic lady in seventeenth-century Scottish portraits, nor did Royalists or Cromwellians adopt any identifiable style. Their accounts make it plain that even the sternest Covenanter among them would spend considerable sums of money each year not only on fine clothing but on jewels, and when these ladies died their bequests usually included the careful transmission of family jewellery to favoured friends and relatives. If such women appear in their portraits devoid of diamonds, rubies and sapphires, it was not because they did not possess any. Their treasures were carefully put aside at home, lying in little wooden and velvet-covered boxes, waiting for the occasions of state when they had to be produced and worn for the honour of the family.

Sometimes, it seems, an item might be too personal and too precious to be worn at all. This would appear to be the most likely explanation of the strange absence of wedding rings in portraits from about 1630 until the early nineteenth century. Various theories have been put forward in the past in an attempt to explain this strange omission from pictures, but none of them is satisfactory. It has been pointed out that there was no place in the Presbyterian marriage service for the exchange of rings, but this is not the determining factor because spousing and wedding rings do appear in portraits of Presbyterian ladies in the decades immediately after the Reformation. It is simply that they have often not been recognised because of their design and their varying position.

Before the Reformation, the wedding ring was always worn on the fourth finger of the right hand because it was believed that a vein ran from that finger direct to the heart. The Reformers may have realised that the text upon which this belief was based contained a mistranslation and that the authority so often quoted had actually said the vein was in the fourth finger of the left hand. Again, they may simply have wished to be different. Whatever the reason, ladies in the pictures of the period 1560-1630 appear with what is unmistakably a wedding ring on the fourth finger of the left hand, on the thumb, or suspended from a fine chain round the neck or even tied to the bandstrings which closed their ruff. The ring was usually gem-set, not so often a plain band, and the stones were frequently arranged in the shape of a heart, sometimes a crowned heart, as may be seen in the portraits of Lady Rothes (14) and the Countess of Winton (8). Once the variable position and the unfamiliar design of such rings is recognised, it is possible to identify wedding or betrothal rings in many portraits of the period.

What became of them after 1630, however? Time and again, respectable wives, mothers of ten, twelve and fourteen children sit sedately in their portraits, their ringless hands arranged artistically in their laps. This is true of ladies of all shades of ecclesiastical opinion, and the documentary evidence makes it clear that they did all have wedding rings. Perhaps it was simply not the custom to wear them. When the Presbyterian Anna, 2nd Marchioness of Hamilton made her will in 1644, amongst the treasured items she bequeathed to her elder son was 'my greit diamont ring. I got it from his father. It is in ane welvet keis [case], and ane lettir of my deir lord's with it.' Similarly, when the Roman Catholic Queen Henrietta Maria died in France in 1669, amongst her most precious possessions in the cabinet by her bedside was a miniature of her husband, Charles I, and 'two rings which are believed to be the Queen's wedding rings'. Perhaps the rings were worn only at the marriage ceremony

detail of 8 Countess of Winton

and then were kept carefully hidden from the public gaze ever after that.

Whatever the explanation, neither wedding ring nor any other kind of ring appears in female portraits of the period. Now unless gloves are worn, it is perfectly possible to display a glittering array of rings without interfering with any garment or accessory. Not so other items of jewellery. They are much more dependent upon the changing fashions of costume and hairstyle. It is not possible to wear short, fancy necklaces when necklines are high and frilly. Bracelets are hidden by long sleeves with deep cuffs. Earrings cannot be seen if it is *de rigueur* to wear a cap tied under the chin. A heavy, gem-set brooch can be worn as a hair ornament only when the hair is brushed back over a pad which provides the necessary support for the gems. Heavy, enamelled jewels which look magnificent against a rich, dark material embroidered with gold thread would seem oppressively out of place beside pale satins. So it is that items of jewellery appear and disappear, complementing the costume of the wearer. With the nineteenth century, heavy crinolines, fussy trimmings and ornate styles were back in fashion once more, along with modesty, propriety and the desire to appear prosperous and respectable. This was a time of sentimentality, too, when hair jewellery commemorating dead relatives was not only given as presents, as it always had been, but now appeared in pictures as well; when widows hung themselves about with enormous necklaces of jet and when the silhouettes and miniatures of husbands and children featured prominently and recognisably in paintings. Perhaps because of Queen Victoria's own devotion to her husband and to married life, wedding rings became necessary accessories in paintings and the now familiar gem-set engagement ring beside a plain wedding band invariably appears on the fourth finger of the left hand.

detail of 42 Princess Marie of Baden

Mass production has increased the range of jewellery available to sitters but in our own century relatively few people sit to an artist for a portrait: a photograph is so much quicker, easier and less expensive. The result is that, when someone does commission a portrait, the old considerations of private affection and public image apply as much as ever they did, because it is a very special occasion. When Lady Forbes sat for her portrait in 1925 (72), she wore her favourite necklace of seed pearls, a gift from her parents, while Mrs Dalyell of the Binns chose her family topazes when she was painted by Stanley Cursiter in 1945 (78).

Interestingly, comparison between the topazes themselves and the picture shows that the artist did not paint them as they really were. He omitted the tiara and devised a huge shoulder ornament which did not really exist. We can only speculate about the alterations made by past artists to the jewels they saw before them. While their predecessors of the sixteenth century took endless trouble to paint what was really there, it is perfectly possible that they invented, or at least enhanced, the flawless pear-drop pearls of the seventeenth century, the elegant little chokers of the eighteenth, or the heavy *parures* of the nineteenth century. Again, some of the dazzling diamonds may really have been paste jewellery, known in Britain from the seventeenth century onwards.

Portraits are not photographs and their painted details cannot be used as evidence in isolation: yet if we look at pictures, read inventories and inspect the brooches, the necklaces and the rings preserved from former centuries, we can learn much about the jewellery of the past, the way it was worn and the motives of the wearers.

ROSALIND K MARSHALL

detail of 78 Mrs Dalyell

THE SIXTEENTH CENTURY

Relatively few Scottish portraits survive from the sixteenth century, but those which do show a wealth of elegant jewellery firmly within the Western European tradition. Goldsmiths clustering round the High Kirk of St Giles in Edinburgh kept abreast of the times. All the contemporary techniques of faceting, foiling, setting, hammering, chasing and enamelling were triumphantly deployed by James Mossman when King James V commissioned him in 1539-40 to remodel the royal crown of Scotland. It can be seen in Edinburgh Castle, and although the design is traditional, the craftsmanship compares with that of London.

The walls of Holyrood Palace were hung with tapestries of scenes from classical myth and history: the Labours of Hercules, the heroism of Perseus, the destruction of Troy and the founding of Rome. This awareness of the humanist culture of the Italian Renaissance is also reflected in his jewellery. James V's caps were laced with aglets (enamelled gold tags) or encircled with bands of jewelled buttons, and they were also pinned with brooches expressing intellectual concepts. Three such badges or 'tergats' listed in his inventory of 1542 were wrought with figurative motifs in relief: a mermaid with diamond tail, 'ane image havand ane dyamont in hir hand and ane gryt rubie under hir feit and a cameo with four rubeis'.

The wardrobe and jewels brought home from France by his daughter Mary, Queen of Scots in 1561 set an example which all well-born women tried to follow. They trimmed their French hoods with jewelled billiments or bands, the stones alternating with pearl clusters as in the one Margaret Seton (1) wears in her hair. Earrings were less important at this period. Most of those shown in portraits are round or pear pearls, either oriental or Scottish, but others were made by goldsmiths. Those listed in the 1566 inventory of the jewels of Mary, Queen of Scots include sapphire drops, shells, little bells and white Jerusalem crosses.

Pendant pearls remained Mary's own favourite style, and when she escaped from Lochleven Castle the prearranged signal to let her know that everything was in readiness for her departure was when one of her servants brought her a pearl earring

detail of Margaret Seton from 1 Lord Seton and Family

which she had 'accidentally' dropped in one of the castle apartments.

No jewel signified status more than the collar or carcanet, richly mounted with gems and pearls in settings of such importance that each link was a jewel in itself. Most prestigious were the collars of the Orders of Chivalry: as a member of the French Order of St Michael, James V had owned four collars wrought with the symbolic shells and knots. Those who did not belong to this exclusive company aspired to wear heavy gold chains with links of various designs, left plain or enamelled. Hans Eworth depicted James, Earl of Moray with a double row of round links across his chest, and in a companion portrait his wife Agnes wears a much more flexible design, plaited so finely she could tie it into a knot.

The less expensive and lighter filigree could contain balls of scented musk or pomander to sweeten the air, with smaller lengths for bracelets at the wrists. Symbols and ciphers could be converted into chains: the Seton chain of ruby Esses and green snakes associated with Queen Mary survives to represent this style. Equally symbolic is the carcanet of ruby double crescent moons and knots with anchor pendant inscribed in Scots HOUP FEIDIS ME, now in the collection of Baron Thyssen-Bornemisza.

The tablets or pendants which hung from jewelled chains or were pinned to the breast and sleeve might, like the hat badges, express classical themes. James V's 'riche targatt with three naikit imagis sett all full of dyamonttis' probably represented the Three Graces, and there was a 'Jewel callit Orpheus' in the collection of Alexander Seton, 1st Earl of Dunfermline. Others were emblems of strength, like the lion, or of Victory, illustrated by the Aberdeen jewel (4).

Miniatures and cameo portraits of illustrious personalities which echo the masterpieces of Raphael, Holbein and Titian were worn as jewels: pendants, tablets, hat-badges and even earrings. Mary, Queen of Scots seems to have given cameos of herself to her friends (2) and other jewels were designed round the heart motif. A crowned amethyst heart sent by James VI to his future wife Anne of Denmark was accompanied by a poem in which the King referred to the magical properties each stone was believed to possess.

Bracelets, almost always worn in pairs, might be studded with gems or mounted with engraved hardstones such as James V's pair, 'sett with gravin rubeis and lytill quyhte heidis [set with engraved rubies and little white heads]'. There were also rows of gold chains held in place by enamelled plaques, like those belonging to Sir James Anstruther, Hereditary Grand Carver to James VI. He wears them in a portrait dated 1591, with other jewels: a splendid suite of mushroom-like buttons, wrought gold belt clasp and two rings.

More rings were made and worn than any other jewel. For business, there were signets engraved with crests and personal ciphers tied together by a lover's knot. While the larger diamonds – point, table, triangle and heart cut – were set as solitaires, the smaller stones were mounted as roses or placed beside a ruby or an emerald. Some designs – hearts, clasped hands and turtle doves – were symbolic of love, while others were reminders of death. A ring set with a sapphire carved as a skull, 'ane small morte head', was in the collection of James V, and there is another type, enamelled, on the finger of Mark Kerr in a portrait of 1551. Like so many Renaissance jewels worn by Scottish men and women it compares with English and continental examples, for what was fashionable in Paris and London was also fashionable in Edinburgh.

DIANA SCARISBRICK

detail of 3 Mary, Queen of Scots

'Amethyst in form of hart
Doth signifie the hart
And constant love unchangeable
That is upon my part
And as the colours of this stone
Are purple mixed with graye
So flames of love my earthlie parts
Consumes me daye by daye
The secret vertues that are hidd
Into this pretious stone
Indues me with meete qualities
For serving such a one.'

1 *George, 5th Lord Seton and his family, by Frans Pourbus, 1572.*

George, 5th Lord Seton, aged thirty-nine, stands amidst his children by his absent wife, Isabel Hamilton: on the left, John and Robert; on the right, Margaret and Alexander. The small boy with the prayer book is William, the youngest of the family. Seton was one of the most devoted servants of Mary, Queen of Scots. This picture was painted in 1572, when he was on a mission to the Spanish Netherlands to try to persuade the Duke of Alva to send an army

to rescue her from captivity, and he is attired as the ambassador of a Roman Catholic queen.

The gold crucifix which hangs from the ribbon round his neck is of the lignum vitae type with arms and upright simulating branches lopped off a tree. He has a jewelled cap band of coloured stones, in high gold collets with chased and enamelled sides, alternating with pairs of pearls. Such a band is called in the inventories the 'cordon of a bonnet'. His brown doublet is fastened by a set of melon-shaped carved crystal buttons

capped with gold and his belt has a wrought gold clasp. On his little finger there are two rings: one has a raised quatrefoil bezel set with a ruby, similar to the jewels in his hat, and the other might be a cameo in an oval bezel.

The pearls entwined in fifteen-year-old Margaret's auburn tresses meet at a ruby jewel. Below it is another with a dark stone – perhaps a sapphire – similarly set and hung with a pearl, which is the centrepiece of a band of pearl clusters, alternating with coloured stones in rich gold settings, mounted on red velvet ribbon. The carcanet round her neck is designed in the same way, except that the pearls between the gold links are set in pairs rather than in clusters of four. From it hangs a pendant jewel with three pearl drops.

The artist has shown the individual pieces in such detail that the portrait could be a pictorial record of Seton possessions. It illustrates standard Renaissance jewellery with yellow gold, soft enamels, diamonds, coloured gems and milky white pearls all having an equal share in the design of each ornament. DS

National Gallery of Scotland

2 *Cameo pendant of Mary, Queen of Scots, late sixteenth century; The Penicuik Necklace, mid-sixteenth century, remodelled in the late seventeenth century.*

The gold outer casing of the pendant is decorated with cloisonné enamel and is set with table-cut diamonds and a native cut ruby. In style it is similar to the group of gold lockets described below (7) and may well be the work of a Scottish goldsmith. At its centre is a chalcedony cameo, of French or Italian work, carved with a bust of Mary, Queen of Scots. The cameo backplate is very high quality enamel, *émail en résille sur verre*, comparable to that on a sixteenth-century French pomander now in the Thyssen-Bornemisza Collection. Although this pendant has no known provenance, it is quite possible that Mary brought several enamel mounted cameos from France in 1561, as gifts for her friends and supporters. Presenting such royal gifts was a well-established means of encouraging loyalty to the Crown. The cameo could then have been incorporated into a Scottish outer case. Immediately before her execution, Mary gave a parting gift of a pair of gold bracelets to one of her servants, Giles Mowbray. This necklace of gold filigree beads, which would originally have held perfume in the form of small balls of musk, was long preserved as an heirloom by the descendants of Giles, the Clerks of Penicuik, and was probably made up from the beads of the original bracelets. GRD

National Museums of Scotland

3 Mary, Queen of Scots, by an unknown artist, about 1610-15, based on a miniature of 1578.

Shown during the years of her captivity in England, Mary wears the sombre outfit which was her habitual costume at that period of her life. Complementing her mourning clothes is jewellery which is equally solemn in character. There is a pearl in her ear, and her neck is encircled by a black chain of hearts and double M's, possibly of glass. A gold crucifix hangs from a black ribbon, and there is a rosary with cross attached at her girdle. A Latin inscription above the table translates: 'Mary by the Grace of God, most pious Queen of Scotland, Dowager of France, in the year of her age and reign 36, of her English captivity 10, year of grace 1578'.

In spite of this date, the portrait derives from a miniature by Nicholas Hilliard, and is believed to have been painted about 1610, as one of a series ordered by James VI. A statute of 1571 forbade the wearing of devotional jewellery of the type depicted: 'ornaments called or named by the name of Agnus Dei, or any crosses, pyctures, beades or such lyke vayne and superstitious thynges from the Bysshop or Sea of Rome'. There seems no doubt, however, that Queen Mary was accustomed to wear them during her final years. When she wrote asking her uncle the Cardinal of Lorraine for jewels to give to her friends, she emphasised that they were not for her, and that she only wore gold crosses. This is confirmed by the inventory of her jewellery drawn up at Chartley in 1586, which specifies 'La croix d'or que Sa Majesté avoit accoustumée de porter, [The gold cross which Her Majesty was in the habit of wearing]'.

Mary owned several valuable rosaries. This one is threaded with black beads, perhaps pomanders alternating with enamelled gold spheres, perhaps 'nuts' enclosing tableaux of Biblical scenes. It hangs from a cross with each arm in the shape of a Gothic S, centred on a roundel enamelled with a picture of The Elders Accusing Susannah, and the inscription ANGUSTIAE UNDIQUE [Troubles on all sides]. There is an obvious parallel between the predicament of Queen Mary and that of Susannah, the innocent heroine of the Apocrypha, saved from execution by Daniel who exposed the conspiracy to destroy her.   DS

Scottish National Portrait Gallery

4 *Jewelled gold pendant with a lock of hair said to be that of Mary, Queen of Scots.*

Known as 'the Aberdeen jewel', the pendant illustrates very well the Renaissance genius for conveying ideas, in this instance the glory of victory, through the art of the goldsmith. A naturalistically enamelled white hand offers a green laurel wreath. On either side, red dragons with long diamond necks emerge from thin linked cornucopiae, each head crowned with a point-cut diamond. From the centre of the laurel wreath hangs a domed crystal locket containing hair said to be that of Mary, Queen of Scots, enclosed in a seven-lobed border, enamelled red. There are twin C scrolls set with point and table-cut diamonds to each side of the wrist, joined by a small line of rubies with a row of opals above them.

The back of the pendant is identical in design, but is ornamented with vari-coloured enamels instead of set with gem-stones; the cornucopiae in bands alternately black and white, the scrolls in black, the dragon necks red and the opals and rubies dark blue and

red respectively. Three round pearls depend from the base.

Two papers are preserved with the pendant, which is an heirloom of the Marquess of Aberdeen. The earliest, in the handwriting of Mary Baillie-Hamilton, wife of George, 5th Earl of Aberdeen, reads: 'Locket with the hair of Mary, Queen of Scots Given by her to one of the Gordon family. Belongs to George'. In 1877 Countess Mary gave the pendant to her daughter-in-law, Ishbel, wife of the 1st Marquess of Aberdeen, who recorded: 'Pendant containing Mary, Queen of Scots hair and said to have been given by her to James Gordon of Methlick on the field of Battle. Given to me to keep as an heirloom by Mary, Countess of Aberdeen, 1877'. James Gordon of Methlick and Haddo (1531-82) was loyal to Queen Mary and is likely to have fought for her at Langside in 1568. There are other examples of the hair of Mary, Queen of Scots, one of them in the collection of Her Majesty The Queen, but none is in a contemporary mount. DS
The Marquess of Aberdeen

5 The Lennox Jewel, about 1564.

This heart-shaped gold locket of complex and fascinating design contains no fewer than twenty-eight emblems and six inscriptions. Traditionally, they are believed to allude to the dangers and difficulties confronting Matthew Stewart, Earl of Lennox and his wife Lady Margaret Douglas. Lennox, exiled from Scotland, had lost all his lands there, and the locket may date from 1564, when he was hoping to regain his ancestral estates. His wife was extremely ambitious both for him and for their elder son, Lord Darnley, whom she was determined to marry to Mary, Queen of Scots. The jewel may have been commissioned by the Countess as a safer means of communication with her husband when he went north. An alternative explanation places the commission in the 1570s, after the murder of Darnley and possibly after Lennox's own assassination. It would then refer to the Countess's desire for vengeance, and her anxieties about the future of her grandson, James VI. Whatever the true significance of this enigmatic piece, its richness of decoration provides ample evidence for speculation. The white border of the heart-shaped gold locket frames four allegorical figures: Faith, Hope, Victory and Truth. Between them is a ruby and emerald crown above a sapphire winged heart with a blue, red and green feather, both concealing devices. Inside the lid of the crown there is a golden lover's knot pierced by two arrows, and two hearts united by a blue buckle inscribed QUAT WE RESOLVE [What we resolve]. A crown is over the cipher MSL [Matthew Stewart Lennox] opposite.

The back of the cover of the winged heart is enamelled with two clasped hands holding a hunting horn on a red string inscribed DEATHE SAL DESOLVE [Death shall dissolve], alluding to the skull and crossbones opposite. An inscription round the back of the locket encloses translucently enamelled emblems, including a crowned salamander in flames, a phoenix, a pelican-in-her-piety, a man seated by a sunflower

with a lizard and a bay tree with a bird in the branches. There are more emblems inside: a burning stake, a woman on a throne, a naked Janus standing on a celestial globe, pulling a woman out of a well, and a devil spitting out flames.

Nothing is known of the history of this extraordinary jewel until it was acquired by Horace Walpole. He treasured it so much that he refused to allow the antiquarian Earl of Buchan to have a drawing made of it for exhibition at the Society of Antiquaries of Scotland in 1792, explaining that 'it is so great a curiosity and cost me such a sum of money...it is so complex and intricate and opens in so many places and the springs and balances are so very small and delicate that when I do show it, which is very rarely, I never let it out of my own hands'. It was acquired for Queen Victoria at the Strawberry Hill sale in 1842.   DS

Reproduced by gracious permission of Her Majesty The Queen

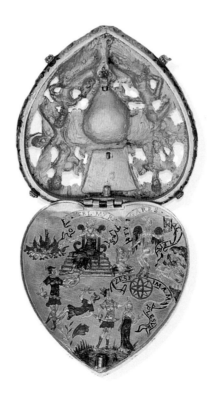

her lace collar is a very important oval pendant with three hanging pearls, the surface studded with diamonds of different cuts and sizes, some of the smaller stones set in clusters. The double rope of pearls interspersed with gold beads at her neck is caught at the centre by a pearl knop where it links up with two chains of pearls with diamonds and falls in four loops down to the waist.

The neck chain has been compared with one recorded in the Eglinton Muniments: 'Ane nek chenze of pearle thred upon thrie cords contening sax [six] gryt knopis of gold enammelit with threttie aucht [thirty eight] small knopes of moos beids coverit with gold', the pearls alternating with groups of the 'moos' beads, which were probably filigree. Her girdle is composed of seed pearls threaded into pillars divided by golden beads and converging on a cylinder from which hangs a ruby pendant. The bracelet beneath the cuff – one of a pair – is studded with gems, some of them diamonds, foiled black. The diamond in the ring on her little finger is held in the setting by black eagle's claws at the corners. All her jewellery looks forward to the seventeenth century, emphasising intrinsic value rather than virtuoso craftsmanship, and conveying the message of wealth rather than intellectual or moral concepts.   DS
Scottish National Portrait Gallery

6 *Lady Agnes Douglas, Countess of Argyll, by an unknown artist, 1599.*

Lady Agnes, one of the seven daughters of the Earl of Morton known for their beauty as 'the seven pearls of Lochleven', is shown here at the age of twenty-five, her expensive black dress providing a wonderful foil for her gold and pearl jewellery.

Her red hair is swept up and padded into a heart-shaped halo, outlined by an attire of seed pearls, and to the right of her brow there is a bodkin with jewelled cluster hanging from a needle. A pear pearl hangs from the jewelled chain in her ear. Pinned to

7 *Three gold and enamelled lockets and two 'earring' miniatures, second half of the sixteenth century.*

All three lockets have late sixteenth-century cloisonné enamel work surrounded by a twisted gold ribbon of seed pearls, and are, or were, each set with two central miniature portraits of figures in late sixteenth-century costume. The locket at the top was said to have been given to an ancestor of the Clerks of Penicuik by Mary, Queen of Scots, and its two portraits were thought to depict Mary with her son, James VI. The damaged locket (which has lost its miniatures) was dug up in

Barnhills Field, near Corsewall Castle, Wigtownshire, while the other belonged to a Scottish family.

The two 'earrings' containing late sixteenth-century miniatures which are set in later gold and crystal mounts were obviously from lockets like the others. They were given to the National Museum by Lord Saltoun in 1784 and are portraits of his ancestors, Sir Alexander Fraser of Philorth (died 1623) and his wife Magdalen Ogilvie (died before 1606). Sir Alexander founded the town of Fraserburgh and tried to establish a university there in 1597.

The similarities in design and workmanship of all three pendants suggest that, if they were not made by the same craftsman, they certainly came from the same workshop. They all have strong Scottish provenances and as there seems to be no direct equivalent from either England or Europe it is possible that they represent a specifically Scottish style of jewellery. While late Renaissance English and European pendants are occasionally set with carved cameos, none exists with this type of miniature portraiture. They may possibly be the 'gold frames for pictures' set with crystals which are so often mentioned in the bills of George Heriot, James VI's jeweller (17).   GRD
National Museums of Scotland

8 Lady Anne Hay, Countess of Winton,
attributed to Adam de Colone, 1625.
Swathed in black, the Countess would at
first sight appear to be clad in widow's
weeds, but her husband was still alive when
this portrait was painted in 1625. The eldest
daughter of Francis, 9th Earl of Erroll, she
had married George, 3rd Earl of Winton in
1609. They had five sons and four daughters
and although five of their family failed to
survive early childhood, none died in 1624-
5, nor did the Earl. He survived his wife,
marrying again after her death in the late
1620s and living on until 1650.

The reason for the Countess's all-enveloping
black remains a mystery, but upon closer
examination it proves to be a most
sumptuous outfit. Round her neck is a very
short string of black beads similar in size to
those seen in the portraits of Mary, Queen
of Scots (3) and Lady Napier (12). It has to
be worn very high because of her expensive
lace ruff. Her delicate pendant earrings are
set with small diamonds, a black ribbon or
cord bow decorating the gold hoop.
Emerging beneath her ruff are further strings
of the tiny black beads, the central loop
supporting a complex diamond jewel. The
neckline of her gown is edged with an ornate
chain composed of diamonds, rubies and
pearls in gold settings, complementing her
gold- and black-embroidered chemise. Her
very buttons are set with diamonds and
rubies, and on her bodice she wears two
splendid pieces. The miniature case pinned
on the right is very plain, but the enormous
aigrette at the other side is studded with
diamonds.

Black beads wound round her wrists form
matching bracelets and on her hands are
diamond rings. The huge heart composed of
diamonds on the fourth finger of her right
hand must be her betrothal or wedding ring.
Next to it, on the small finger, is the popular
type of pointed diamond traditionally used
for inscribing initials or verses on glass
windows, while on her left hand she has a
large diamond surrounded by smaller ones.
This is the jewellery of a very wealthy lady
indeed. RKM
Scottish National Portrait Gallery

9 The 'Memorial Jewel' of Margaret Keith,
possibly first half of the seventeenth century.
This garnet jewel is traditionally associated
with Margaret, daughter of Sir Alexander
Keith of Ludquhairn. She was born about
1580 and married George Graeme of
Inchbrackie in 1608. The couple were on the
Royalist side during the Civil War and were
related to the Marquis of Montrose. George
was imprisoned by the Covenanters in 1641,
during which time his estates were raided
and plundered. Margaret, a spirited lady,
tried to protect the family fortunes as best
she could.

One story relates that she was unable to
prevent the theft by Lord Balcarres of her
husband's favourite grey mare. Knowing
that George 'lovit the beist' [loved the beast],
she tried to bargain with Balcarres at the
Covenanters' camp at Balloch. She offered
him her own horse in exchange, but such
was the Covenanters' contempt for her that

they stole her horse too and forced her to
walk ten miles home.

Her curiously made jewel has very rubbed
cabochon and table-cut 'pendalique'
almandine garnets in distinctive silver
settings, which show signs of having been
altered. The twisted wire filigree interspersed
with plain silver studs and the toothed
collets are, however, similar to those of the
Lochbuie Brooch and the Glenorchy
Charmstone (20). Although it may have
been altered at a later date, it seems possible
that this is basically an early seventeenth-
century pendant or, more likely, a breast
jewel made by a local silversmith or *ceard* to
imitate the more elaborate fashionable
jewels of the period. GRD
National Museums of Scotland

10 *Lady Anne Livingston, Countess of Eglinton, by an unknown artist, about 1612.* Lady Anne is shown in court dress with a wealth of lavish jewellery. Above her brow is a large jewelled bodkin which may be the 'greit jewell conteining fourtene greit dyamondis with fyne pendant triangill dyamondis' which she bequeathed to her son Hew, Lord Montgomerie. From the gold ring in her ear hangs a ribbon bow-knot with a finger ring attached. Round her neck she has a choker of large pearls and a black cord with a stone in a narrow enamelled frame, with a pear pearl pendant lying just above her breast.

Tied to a ribbon bow-knot hangs a miniature case (11) with diamond-set crowned cipher CAR and Esses, a pear pearl below. Lady Anne wears this above her heart, as does Queen Anne in her portraits by Van Somer and Marcus Gheeraerts. The case was a mark of regard from the Queen, after whom Lady Anne may have been named and whose service she entered as Maid of Honour in 1605.

King James VI promised her father, the Earl of Linlithgow, that he would provide a dowry for her, but in the event this promise was forgotten. Instead, the Queen gave her jewels from her own great collection, inherited from Queen Elizabeth. On a visit home to Scotland in 1607, the Queen also gave Lady Anne a 'faire pear pearl pendant with a stalk of gold through it among other jewels to hang at a jewel' (perhaps that depicted in the portrait), a ruby and diamond pendant of the Annunciation, and two chains, one of knots of different types and sizes, the other of pearls interspersed with pomanders.

The miniature case was a special purchase from George Heriot and so it had not come from the Queen's own collection. It could have been a wedding present given in 1612 when Lady Anne married Sir Alexander Seton of Foulstruther, later 6th Earl of Eglinton, from whom the miniature descended until sold by the family in 1922. DS

A Private Collection

11 *Queen Anne of Denmark jewelled miniature case, about 1610.*

The miniature case worn by Lady Anne Livingston in her portrait (10) is preserved to this day in the Fitzwilliam Museum, Cambridge. Its translucent red cover is embellished with table-cut diamonds set in four collets, two Esses, a double C, and Anne of Denmark's personal cipher, CAR crowned. Another diamond is set in a collet placed lozenge-wise beneath the suspension loop. The back is also enamelled red with white crowned double A cipher, two Esses and white border with pea-pod trails. The inside of the cover is hatched with addorsed C scrolls and stylised foliage.

Contained within the case is a little picture of the Queen, from the studio of Nicholas Hilliard. This was the great age of the jewelled picture box or miniature case. Those ordered by Anne of Denmark from George Heriot are of various designs: 'a rose jewel opening for a picture', a 'jewel in fashion of a bay leaf opening for a picture set with diamondis' and in 1611 a 'tablet with cipher A and C set on the one side with

diamonds'. This date also coincides with the style of dress worn by the Queen in the miniature itself.

Whereas the Cs could refer to the Queen's brother, Christian IV of Denmark to whom she was devoted, and her son, the future Charles I, the Esses are more enigmatic. Since it is uncrowned, the S is unlikely to recall her mother, Sophie of Mecklenberg, and it could signify Sovereign or Souvenir, a traditional interpretation from the fifteenth century onwards. Esses were used by Queen Anne in her correspondence and in a letter to George Villiers of 1616 she places an S immediately after the personal pronoun. At the end, after her signature ANNA R, there are five more Esses.

The miniature belongs to the group of jewels with which loyal Scottish families were rewarded for their support by the Stewarts in the early years of their accession to the throne of England. An heirloom of the Earls of Eglinton and Winton, it was sold, with another of James VI and I, by Christie's on 13 July 1922. DS

The Fitzwilliam Museum

detail of 16 'Lady Mary Douglas'

II

THE SEVENTEENTH AND EIGHTEENTH CENTURIES

In June 1603, Queen Anne of Denmark left Edinburgh to follow her husband south to his new capital. Henceforth, the court would be in London and in that city Anne would dazzle with her elaborate frounced farthingale petticoats, her rich masquing costumes and her taste for innovative jewellery. No matter how distant the court might be, fashions were always court fashions, and so Scotswomen now looked to London for the latest styles, relying on husbands and friends to send them details of what they should be wearing.

Throughout James VI's sojourn in the south, Spanish fashions were in vogue, with dark colours, sumptuous effects and heavy jewellery. By his later years, however, ladies were tiring of these old-established looks. The art of stone-cutting was developing rapidly on the continent. It was no longer necessary to enhance small, table-cut diamonds with large, enamelled settings. Gems were beginning to glisten and flash, and so the setting became no more than the means of displaying the jewels instead of being the dominant element in the design. Neckchains became lighter, settings almost flower-like and black silk cords suddenly found a place in jewellery.

At first they appear in conjunction with ruff ornaments and pendants: trailing from the ruff jewel or suspending the gems round the neck. In this form they are unexceptional, but in the paintings of Cornelius Jonson, William Larkin, Paul van Somer and others they take different, more fantastical styles. Sometimes the black silk is wound four or five times round each wrist instead of a bracelet, and quite often the lowest strand of silk is attached to a ring on one of the fingers.

In theory, these cords might have been a way of making sure that a precious ring could not be lost, but they are not always associated with gems and it is clear that they were a decorative feature in themselves. They develop purely ornamental loops, and in this context earrings begin to take on even more bizarre forms, with black silk bows, pendant gems hung from cords threaded through small gold hoops and heraldic, religious and other devices (16). At the same time, jewelled plumes appear in the hair. These aigrettes and the accompanying earstrings enjoyed a brief period of popularity.

24

Unknown before 1610, they have disappeared again completely by the mid 1630s.
By then, Britain had a new Queen, for in 1625 Charles I married the French princess
Henrietta Maria. She was the daughter of Marie de Medici, a lady renowned for the
splendour of her jewels and her astuteness in haggling with the merchants who came
to sell them to her. Henrietta was brought up to know all about precious stones, and
from childhood she possessed her own goldsmith to look after her gems. When she
first arrived in England she was wearing the traditional heavy brocades and intricate
jewelled chains. Encouraged by her husband, however, she put away her
uncomfortable, thickly patterned farthingales and turned instead to pale silks and
satins cut on softer lines. She allowed her natural curls to hang down to her shoulders,
and when she sat for her portrait she did not put on her fabulous diamonds. Instead,
she wore a simple pearl necklace and a pair of beautiful pendant pearl earrings.
Throughout the 1630s, Charles continued to shower her with gems, but the image he
and she chose to convey in their many portraits, first by Daniel Mytens and then by Sir
Anthony van Dyck, was one of elegant simplicity, and soon, of course, everyone else
followed suit. A Scottish lady, like her English counterparts, would wind a string of
pearls through her hair, fasten another string round her neck, hang from her ears the
biggest pearls she could find and keep her diamond rings and necklaces in her cabinet.
There is no doubt that the Scotswomen of the period possessed such treasures. They
were continually going to Edinburgh to goldsmiths like Conrad Etinger or George
Main to have heirlooms re-set in modern manner or to purchase new rings and clips
and clasps. It was simply that the conventions of portraiture precluded these
valuables from being displayed, and so although occasionally one glimpses a
magnificent diamond and ruby jewel like the one worn by the Countess of Cassillis in
her hair (23), for the most part fine pearls, real or imagined, are almost the only
personal ornaments seen in paintings.

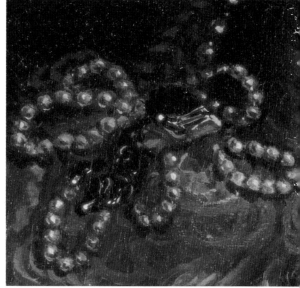

detail of 23 Countess of Cassillis

Moreover, as the century progressed, styles became increasingly severe until a modest
pearl button at the neck of the chemise was the one jewel visible in women's pictures.
Not until the 1720s did the desire for ornamentation revive once more, and then it
took a rather different form. Instead of bringing out their neglected gems, ladies
enthused over pretty, frivolous accessories: frothy lace cuffs cascading from elbow-
length sleeves, glossy ribbon bows sewn to the bodice, enchanting little ruffs or black
velvet bands worn round the neck, posies of artificial flowers tucked into the neckline
or perched on the head. Older ladies concealed their hair and their ears with frilled
caps tied under the chin and modestly hid their necklines with voluminous kerchiefs.
They all possessed fine jewellery of course, but there was scarcely anywhere to put it
amidst such an abundance of fancy trimmings.
Pearls never entirely lost their painted popularity, however, and in the second half of
the century, chokers suddenly found favour instead of, or occasionally with, the
black velvet neckbands. Now, in portraits by Allan Ramsay and his contemporaries,
we see three, four and even more short strings of pearls worn high on the neck and
fastened behind with a huge silk bow which very often matched the wearer's dress.
These chokers went well with the neat little head, the pointed bodice and the hooped
skirt then in fashion, and the proximity of the pearls to the face undoubtedly had a
flattering effect. By the 1790s, however, even they had almost vanished as instead
women draped themselves in gauzy, chemise-style gowns and thought it most elegant
to appear with no jewellery at all.   ROSALIND K MARSHALL

12 Margaret Graham, Lady Napier,
attributed to Adam de Colone, 1626.
The famous Marquess of Montrose's red-
haired sister Margaret stands by a velvet-
covered table, a feather fan in her hand.
Seven years earlier, she had married
Archibald, 1st Lord Napier, who described
her as 'a woman religious, chaste and
beautiful, and my chief joy in this world'.
She was pregnant with her second daughter,
Lilias, when this portrait was painted but
her outfit is the height of elegance, her black
gown not only enriched with embroidery
and fine lace but complemented by a
fascinating array of jewels.

On her head is an aigrette, a plume worn
from a gem-set band, the pearl edging
almost resembling lace in its intricacy.
Beneath her bushy hair we glimpse a small
gold hoop through which a black silk cord is
threaded with the initial S, one from each
ear. Pinned to her lace collar is a delicate
ornament of diamonds and pearls, a pelican
feeding her young. The pelican was believed
to wound her own breast so that her blood
would nourish her offspring. The bird
therefore became a symbol of Christ and his
charity and was a favourite motif in
Renaissance jewellery. A gold brooch of the
pelican-in-her-piety dating from the fifteenth

century was found in the River Meuse and is
now in the British Museum; the Victoria and
Albert Museum has a gold pendant from
sixteenth-century Spain. It is a little
surprising to find the fervently Presbyterian
Lady Napier wearing such a jewel, but it
may have been a family heirloom.
The long chains worn round her shoulders
and caught up on her bodice have pearls in
enamelled gold settings and the large jewel
pinned to the centre of her neckline is set
with many small diamonds. Another
diamond brooch is pinned to the lace edge of
her neckline. Round her neck is a series of
very fine gold chains with small diamonds at
intervals, and on each wrist she has a triple
string of amber beads. A delicate pearl-set
bracelet is worn over each cuff. The one on the
left is scarcely visible because the area of hand
and wrist was at one time damaged, before
the picture came into the Scottish National
Portrait Gallery's collection. It has since been
restored. Both hands are ringless. RKM
Scottish National Portrait Gallery

a   b

d

e

c

13 *Collection of chains, and a diamond necklace, about 1600.*

These chains, which are extremely rare, were made for a prosperous Edinburgh merchant about 1600 and have remained in the same family ever since. Although chains were worn by both men and women in the sixteenth century, by this date they were going out of fashion for men, who did however expect to give and receive them as official and diplomatic gifts. Women continued to wear them, and the number which have survived in the Cheapside Hoard at the Museum of London indicates that they were still in fashion by the mid-seventeenth century. These present chains are not as delicate as those in the Cheapside Hoard, and their asymmetrical foliate design and trails of white dots indicate a date of about 1600-10.

The chains (e) illustrate several types of link. One is composed of twenty-five openwork links, thirteen of them of asymmetrical design with traces of black, dotted with white centred on a white cross, alternating with twelve round double-sided links with black scrolls radiating out from a white cruciform centre. The hook plate is enamelled with black scrolls and white symmetrical ornament.

Two bracelets (a, b) are each composed of five oval openwork links of blue, green and black dotted with white flowers, the petals

and narrow leaves radiating out from a central cluster, alternating with four blue, black, white and green openwork discs bordered with foliate scrolls.

There is also a chain (c) composed of fourteen red octofoils each with a central ring framed in circles with black spots between, alternating with thirteen red and white crosses.

The enamelled gold necklace (d) is composed of sixteen links of broken black scrollwork and leaves, each set with a diamond in a thick square collet surmounted by a crown which is green, blue and black with white dots. The necklace is hung with a fringe of pendants each set with a table-cut diamond in a petal-shaped collet. The openwork centre-piece is larger, with five diamonds set into a cross and a sixth hanging below, set lozengewise, with black leaves curved round the collet. The necklace is attached to thin gold chains which fasten at the back.

The individual links, each with a crown, (except for the centre-piece and fringe of pendants) are simplified versions of a design by Corvinianus Saur of Augsburg, invited to Copenhagen by Christian IV in 1596 and appointed court goldsmith in 1613. The necklace has the same provenance as the chains and is likely to have been made by the same goldsmith, being similar in both technique and style.   DS

A Private Collection

14 *Lady Anne Erskine, Countess of Rothes and her daughters Mary and Margaret, by George Jamesone, 1626.*

In a splendid black and gold dress, the Presbyterian Lady Rothes stands by a table, a pendant spilling negligently from the coffer beside her right hand. There is a jewelled plume in her hair and she wears earrings of intriguing design.

In the early years of the seventeenth century, earrings often took strange and fantastic forms. Writing in 1609, the poet Samuel Rowlands mocked the young dandies who wore a shoelace dangling from one ear, a fashion followed by the Queen herself. Van Somer painted Anne of Denmark in her riding habit, with a shoelace in her left ear. Her daughter, Elizabeth of Bohemia, preferred to thread a long narrow plait of hair, perhaps belonging to her husband, through a gold hoop beside a small crowned heart.

Scottish ladies did this too. There is a miniature of Juliana Kerr with just such a plait, while Lady Rothes favoured a long, narrow coil of hair in one ear with black silk cords and tiny pendants in the other. A large diamond brooch is fastened to the centre of her neckline, a diamond-studded miniature case is pinned to her bodice, she has bracelets on each wrist and she wears a gem-set ring in the shape of a heart, probably her betrothal or wedding ring.

Her daughters, six-year-old Mary (on the left) and five-year-old Margaret, both have gem-set billiments on their heads and wear coral necklaces. Imported from Italy and other Mediterranean countries, coral had long been valued for its supposedly magical properties. Since it was believed to protect its wearer against evil spells, it was often made into jewellery for children. Adults wore coral too, of course, and Margaret, Countess of Findlater's list of valuables in 1705 included a coral necklace worth two pounds seven shillings Scots.

The Countess of Rothes lived until 1641. Mary married a leading Covenanter and had seven children. Margaret was three times married and had six sons, all of whom died in infancy, and six daughters.   RKM

Scottish National Portrait Gallery

15 *Selection of rings, fifteenth century to seventeenth century.*

No jewel brings us more closely in contact with the daily lives of our ancestors than the ring. This group is particularly evocative, for it comprises rings used for business, for marriage, to show religious belief and perhaps sorrow in bereavement.

The earliest signet is the bronze (once gilt) ring with oblong bezel bearing a Gothic letter H, crowned, between two palm branches (a). Found in Dunblane Cathedral during restoration work in 1918, it compares with many other fifteenth- and early sixteenth-century signets used by those private individuals who were neither entitled to bear arms nor were members of merchant guilds. They sealed documents with the initial of their own Christian or surname instead.

The mid-sixteenth-century gold ring with disc bezel roughly inscribed IQ/MF within a beaded border might also have been a signet, with the two pairs of initials representing a man and his wife (b). The round bezel of the third inscribed ring bears the Sacred Monogram IHS, an abbreviation of the Greek name of Christ (c). It was

found in 1825, during the excavation of an old graveyard near Arbroath, but similar devotional rings have also been found south of the border. They are all modest versions of the splendid diamond pendants of the Sacred Monogram listed in the inventories of the Tudor and Jacobean queens and worn by Jane Seymour and Anne of Denmark in portraits.

Three different types of wedding ring are represented. Two are silver 'fede' rings (from the Latin word for trust), with bezels formed of hands clasped or united in love (d, e). The motif has a long history and the earliest recorded example in Britain was found in a hoard at Larkhill, with coins dating from the twelfth century. The posy ring or plain gold band (f) is inscribed QUHAIR THIS I GIUE I UISS TO LIUE [Where this is give I wish to live]. Such posies, or rhyming inscriptions, might have been composed by the couple themselves or with the help of friends and families.

The richest people liked a diamond wedding ring, for the impenetrable stone allied to the circle of the ring, emblematic of eternity, signified a love that would endure for ever. This was why Mary, Queen of Scots was wedded to Lord Darnley with a diamond ring, and in her will of 1566, made just before the birth of their son, the future James VI, she left it to him. Hers was red, but this example (g) is enamelled in blue, red and white. It was dug up in a field at Turnberry, Ayrshire.

According to tradition Queen Mary wore the black enamelled, flower-like opal cluster ring (h) in mourning for her husband Francis II of France when he died in 1560. There is no documentary evidence, nor are there contemporary parallels with the design, but opals do occur in surviving sixteenth-century jewels and the quality of this one is excellent. The claw-like settings, however, suggest a later date. They are reminiscent of those used to hold opals in the magnificent Grenville Jewel of about 1635-40. DS

National Museums of Scotland

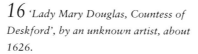

16 'Lady Mary Douglas, Countess of Deskford', by an unknown artist, about 1626.

Earstrings did not always consist of shoelaces or plaited hair. In this portrait, they are black silk cords terminating in little symbols. The significance of the cross is obvious and the other emblems must have had religious, heraldic or sentimental connotations of their own.

Next to the cross in this lady's right ear is a crowned black heart with a large gold S above it. Initials had been a favourite motif in jewellery design since at least the mid-fifteenth century. Sometimes they were the letters which stood for Jesus Christ, IHS, as seen in paintings of Henry VIII's wife Jane Seymour and in portraits of Anne of Denmark.

Often, the owner used his own initial. Henry II of France possessed a large H set with a diamond and fine ruby. He gave it to Mary, Queen of Scots when she married his son. Anne of Saxony in the 1560s had several pendants in the shape of the letter A and when Queen Caterina of Sweden died in 1583 a crowned C set with rubies was one of the items of jewellery placed in her tomb. Alternatively, the initial might be that of the donor. Anne of Denmark is often seen in pictures with a jewelled C4, the gift of her brother King Christian IV.

The other symbols worn by the present sitter are probably heraldic. The crowned red heart is the well-known emblem of the Earls of Morton and a crescent features prominently in the coat of arms of the Scott family. This lady has traditionally been known as Mary Douglas, Countess of Deskford, daughter of William, 6th Earl of Morton and his wife Helen Scott. The emblems would seem to support this identity but since Mary married in 1582 she would have been in her fifties at least when the picture was painted: the costume places it firmly in the 1620s. As this sitter is clearly a much younger woman, her identity is tantalisingly withheld from us, and along with it the true meaning of her earstrings. RKM

A Private Collection

school which bears his name, than it does to his work as a craftsman. There is not a single piece still in existence with his maker's mark, and only one or two jewels can confidently be ascribed to his workshop (11). We do know, however, that he made and supplied a large amount of jewellery for the royal family, especially for Anne of Denmark. It was principally on this royal patronage, and his role as money-lender to James VI and I and Anne, that his vast fortune rested. In 1609, for example, the Queen herself owed him some £18,000 sterling.

Born in 1563, Heriot had been apprenticed to his father, also an Edinburgh goldsmith, and was admitted to the Edinburgh Incorporation of Goldsmiths in 1588. He later became Deacon of the Incorporation and Deacon Convener of the Trades on the Town Council.

This rise to prominence continued when he was appointed Goldsmith to the Queen in 1597 and then Jeweller to the King in 1601. On James's accession to the English throne, Heriot followed him to London. Thereafter his business continued to flourish and on his death in 1623 he left the staggering sum of over £50,000 sterling. Almost half of it went to endow a charitable institution for the sons of 'decayed burgesses of Edinburgh'.

There is some doubt about the identity of the artist of this portrait. The court artist Paul van Somer painted a portrait of Heriot in London which was apparently brought to Edinburgh on the instructions of one of Heriot's executors in 1637. The statue which now adorns the courtyard of the school was supposedly modelled from it. It is thought that the Edinburgh artist John Scougal also used the Van Somer as the source for this painting. GRD

The Governors of George Heriot's Trust

17 *George Heriot, attributed to John Scougall, copy of a portrait of about 1615.* George Heriot is perhaps Scotland's best-known goldsmith/jeweller. However, his fame owes more to the immortality bestowed on him by Sir Walter Scott in *The Fortunes of Nigel* (where the nickname 'Jinglin Geordie' first appears), and to his charitable endowment of the Edinburgh

18 *The Duchess of Atholl's diamond cross, about 1690.*

Jewelled crosses are rarely seen in portraits, nor are they often mentioned in inventories until the last decades of the seventeenth century. There was 'a great cross of diamonds containing five bigg ones in the middle and set about with smaller ones of several sizes' in the collection of jewellery bequeathed by the Countess of Lauderdale in 1671, and it may have resembled this gold cross, once worn by the Duchess of Atholl. Set with rose-cut diamonds, it has a central oval collet flanked by two others placed horizontally for the arms, and by one above and two below on the vertical axis for the upright. Four smaller stones in collets hatched with double lines radiate out from the centre between the arms. Above the suspension loop there is another diamond in an oval collet with four loops at the sides through which a black ribbon passes. This is a runner, or coulan, by which the position of the cross could be adjusted. First mentioned at Versailles in 1688, runners were thereafter recorded in British inventories such as that listing the stock of the London jeweller Michael Wilson in 1709: 'a string of diamonds, runner and cross'.

The rose-cut diamonds, and the vandyked, indented ornament on the substantial gold settings epitomise the seventeenth-century style of jewellery. It is a rare survival, for the next generation broke up ornaments of this kind, recutting the larger diamonds as brilliants for resetting in new, lighter designs executed in silver rather than gold, to avoid yellow reflections.   DS

From His Grace the Duke of Atholl's Collection at Blair Castle, Perthshire

19 *John, 1st Lord Belhaven and his wife, Margaret Hamilton, from the studio of Sir Anthony van Dyck, about 1638.*

Lady Belhaven, sitting serenely with the husband she was to save from arrest and probable death during the Civil War, wears jewellery typical of her time: the string of pearls woven through her hair, the huge pendant pearl earrings, the short pearl necklace and the elaborate jewelled clasps. The illegitimate daughter of the 2nd Marquess of Hamilton, she had been acknowledged by him and had been brought up with his family as a wealthy, aristocratic lady. Apart from possessing fine jewellery, Lady Belhaven had a particular interest in charms and amulets. Skilled in nursing and the preparation of herbal remedies, she was consulted for medical advice by a wide circle of friends and relatives, and although she was a staunch Presbyterian she was willing to enlist the help of the supernatural, upon occasion. When her great-niece Margaret, Countess of Panmure suffered a series of miscarriages, Lady Belhaven lent her a bloodstone in a little silk bag, with the hope that 'it may be as effectual to serve Your Ladyship as it has proved to others'. Lady Panmure was to wear it from a ribbon round her waist, and round her neck she was to suspend an eagle's stone, which Lady Belhaven also supplied. This curiously named substance, in fact a hard piece of oxide of iron, was widely believed to have curative properties. RKM
Scottish National Portrait Gallery

20 *Charmstones: The Glenorchy Charmstone; the charmstone of the Stewarts of Ardsheal; the Mackenzie of Ardloch charmstones.*

The belief that certain curious stones or other unusual objects had supernatural powers was an ancient one. In Scotland, particularly in the Highlands, such charms and amulets were prized as talismans against witchcraft and the evil-eye, and were especially used for curing illness, both in human beings and animals. Just as Lady Belhaven had a stone which she believed had curative powers (see 19), the Earl Marischal kept 'ane jasp [jasper] stane for stemming of blood' in a small coffer along with all his most precious jewels, valuing it at 500 French crowns, a very considerable sum in 1622.

Balls and ridged pieces of rock crystal were also thought to have strong healing powers, and were frequently set in early reliquaries and brooches, such as St Fillan's Crozier and the Lochbuie Brooch. They were often mounted or bound in silver, a metal which was also supposed to have medicinal properties. Some were suspended from chains so that they could be dipped into water, which was then drunk or sprinkled on the sufferer. Although not strictly speaking jewellery, these stones were highly regarded and jealously preserved by the families with whom they were associated. One of the most famous charmstones (top right), that of the Campbell family of Glenorchy and Breadalbane, does seem to have been worn by at least one of its owners. The ridged crystal is set in silver which is decorated with four coral studs and four smaller silver studs on twisted wire collars. Its construction is somewhat similar to the Lochbuie Brooch and even to the Margaret Keith 'Memorial' Jewel (9). It is described in a Breadalbane inventory of 1640 as 'ane stane of the quantitie of half ane hen's eg set in silver...quilk [which] Sir Coline Campbell first Laird of Glenurchy woir quhen he faucht in battale at the Rhodes agaynst the Turks, he being one of the Knychtis [Knights] of the Rhodes'. Such stones were often lent or hired out to those who had need of them, and people are recorded as having travelled up to a hundred miles to procure their aid.   GRD
National Museums of Scotland

21 *Lady Mary Stewart, by an unknown artist, 1658.*

Lady Mary Stewart is shown half length, her corkscrew curls covered by a black net hood. A red ribbon bow-knot can be seen pinned to the white coif under the hood and others stand out on her bodice. Their bright colour is echoed by the beads of her bracelets, one on her wrist and the other as yet unfastened. Strung in two rows, the beads are most likely to be coral, but they could also be of reddish gold amber, or cornelian, all of which were recorded in the inventories of private individuals and of merchants' stock in the middle years of the seventeenth century.

A Cambridge don, Thomas Nicols, explained the various properties of these substances in *A Lapidary or the History of Pretious Stones* (1652). According to him, coral was considered the most beautiful and, if worn as an amulet, would 'drive away fears, keep men from enchantments, from poysoning, from epilepsies, and from the insultings of devils, from thunder, and from tempests and from all manner of perills'. He says that rare and precious amber was liked not only for its transparent colour, but because it 'breatheth forth the fragrant smells of odiferous spices'. As for cornelian, Nicols observed that it was used chiefly in seals and for ornaments for the neck, wrists and hair of women, being a 'good protection against witchcrafts and fascinations and was of value for its own beauty'.

The golden apple in Lady Mary's hand might be a pomander to sweeten the air: it is attached to an ornamental tag seen between the left thumb and index finger. DS
National Museums of Scotland

22 *The Carruthers Jewel, first half of the seventeenth century.*

This gold and enamelled box or pendant is set on one side with an early seventeenth-century miniature of a rather voluptuous lady under a piece of rock crystal, surrounded by crudely table-cut emeralds, amethysts and garnets. The other side consists of a banded agate cameo carved with the figure of a saint, an angel and a dragon, possibly representing St George and the Dragon. Again this is surrounded by table-cut amethysts, garnets and emeralds. Both sides form hinged lids, one of which opens to reveal a light blue enamelled box, divided into six compartments. The lid of this inner box has a central pink rose on blue enamel with six radiating sections, painted with the letters 'N.B; R.B; S.B; K.B; M.B'. Family tradition states that it was 'the Family Jewel' of the Carruthers of Holmains in Dumfriesshire, who used it as a Roman Catholic reliquary. Although it does seem to have descended from the Carruthers family to Lord Elibank, who presented it to the National Museum in 1973, there is no real evidence to suggest that it was a reliquary. The nature of the miniature also makes this unlikely, and indeed the Holmains family in the seventeenth century were Presbyterians. It is far more probable that it is a cosmetic box and that the initials inside relate to the types of preparations contained in each of the compartments. GRD
National Museums of Scotland

23 *Susanna Hamilton, Countess of Cassillis, by J M Wright, 1662.*

Susanna was the younger daughter of the 1st Duke of Hamilton, Charles I's principal Scottish adviser. Her early years were disrupted by the Civil War and she spent part of her adolescence in France with her grandmother, at the court of Charles's exiled Queen, Henrietta Maria. This is probably why no marriage was arranged for her. In normal circumstances a great heiress's family would have found her a husband by the time she was sixteen but when Susanna returned to London and had this portrait painted she was twenty-nine and still single.

Her ivory silk dress is set off by the elegant pearl jewellery fashionable at the court of Charles II: hair ornament, pendant earrings, necklace and breast jewel. A lady wore her hair in a small bun at the back of the head, as in former years, but instead of allowing loose curls to flow naturally to the shoulders, she now favoured corkscrew ringlets bunched up at either side of the face and supported on concealed wires.

With this new fashion came a new style in jewellery. A long string of pearls was placed across the top of the head and arranged in loops resembling bows on each bunch of wired-out side curls. The pearls were kept in place with bodkins, often with small, jewelled heads. Susanna's pearl bow, however, is tethered by a magnificent ruby and diamond jewel, probably adapted from a breast ornament. The breast jewel worn in this picture is partly concealed by the sitter's diaphanous scarf but it is obviously an intricate piece, with pendant pearls and a string of fine pearls looped up through small gold hoops. The front of her dress itself appears to be enriched with sliced diamonds. Soon after the portrait was painted, Lady Susanna returned to Scotland. When she was thirty-six years old she finally married. Her husband was the impoverished young Earl of Cassillis, who was just nineteen. She spent the rest of her life on his Ayrshire estates, bore him a son and a daughter and finally died in 1694 at the age of sixty-one. RKM
Scottish National Portrait Gallery

c

a

24 *Selection of Charles I commemorative jewellery, second half of the seventeenth century.*

Charles I was beheaded by his Parliamentarian enemies on 30 January 1649, on a scaffold in front of his Banqueting House in Whitehall. Women attending the execution mopped up every drop of the spilt royal blood, and pieces of the linen kerchiefs they used soon became prized relics of the King. From the very outset, Charles's supporters saw his death as a kind of martyrdom, and used its imagery in the Royalist Cause. A vast number of mementos and pieces of jewellery was produced to commemorate the 'Martyr King' and to encourage faith in the cause, whose figurehead was now the youthful Charles II.

Some Royalist jewellery incorporated fragments of Charles I's bloodsoaked shirt, locks of his hair or simply miniature portraits of him. They ranged in quality from the crude silver lockets with Charles's cypher (a) to very fine gold and enamel rings set with beautifully achieved portraits, all the more astonishing for their tiny dimensions. The one shown here (b) is set with a superb brilliant-cut diamond. Although such complicated cuts were being produced by seventeenth-century jewellers, they were more common in the next century, so it is possible that this diamond is a later replacement for a crystal.

Perhaps one of the most unusual mementos of the King is the gold pendant set with nine crudely table-cut diamonds (c). The central diamond covers the royal initials 'CR' in gold wire set on a pad of cloth and a lock of hair, which may be relics of the King. GRD
National Museums of Scotland

25 *Gold and enamel flower spray, mid-seventeenth century.*

This is a beautiful, possibly unique, example of a 'trembler' jewel. The three enamelled flower heads (one of which is set with eight table-cut emeralds) are attached to the main stem by fine spiral wires, which allow them to move, or 'tremble', imitating the movement of natural flowers. The stem has two loops for attaching the jewel either to clothing or possibly for use as a hair ornament.

The quality of the enamelling is very fine, although the blue ground on the back of the top flower is slightly fragmentary. However, the most remarkable element in this piece is the tiny yet accomplished miniature depicting the head and shoulders of King Charles I, set under a crystal in the centre of the pink rose. It is no more than five millimetres across.

Unfortunately there is no documented provenance before 1910 for the spray. Colonel Le Rossignol, who bequeathed it to the National Museum along with a magnificent collection of Stewart jewellery, bought it in 1910. At that time 'it was said to have been given by Charles himself and since to have been handed down in one family till quite recently'. An article in 1923 also mentions that it 'may be that this is one of the four or five such ornaments executed to the order of King Charles for presentation to his own particular friends, and in our knowledge the only one that has come to light'. GRD
National Museums of Scotland

b

26 *Lady Jean Hay, Countess of March, by David Scougall, about 1668.*

Not only adult ladies and gentlemen wore their best clothes and fine jewellery when they sat for their portraits: this picture shows a young girl in sophisticated and elegant attire. Lady Jean Hay, daughter of the Marquess of Tweeddale, was only thirteen when her portrait was painted. She still has a child's fine lace apron, with the bib pinned to the front of her dress, but otherwise her garments and her jewels are those of a grown-up lady. Pearls are looped up on her wired-out side curls and in each ear she wears a very large pearl drop. Earrings of this kind had become extremely popular during the second quarter of the seventeenth century. It was difficult to find two beautiful pearls which matched each other in size, colour and shape and so earrings such as these were much prized. Very few are still in existence. This is partly because pearls deteriorate with the passage of time but also because, like other jewels, they were often re-used in different settings. The pearl drop earring worn by Charles I on the day of his execution still exists in a private collection, but that is exceptional and the only pair of really fine pearl earrings of the period which are known today were a set given by Louis XIV to his mistress Marie Mancini. Pendant pearls remained popular as part of brooches and Lady Jean's, which is a circle set with diamonds, features three large pearl drops. Her portrait has been attributed to David Scougall, and if this is correct it must have been painted in Edinburgh in the mid 1660s. The attribution appears to be borne out by a receipt dated 10 March 1668, when Lady Jean's mother paid the artist six pounds sterling 'for the two children's pictures'. A few weeks later, Lady Jean went to England, only to die of smallpox at the age of fourteen. RKM

Lady Daphne Stewart

27 *Selection of rings, seventeenth century to eighteenth century.*

The 'fede' or clasped hand ring with its promise of fidelity remained in use long after the medieval period. During the Renaissance it was combined with another symbol, the heart, enamelled red and flaming with the fires of love (a). Similar heart and hand rings were bought by Anne of Denmark from George Heriot and are recorded in his accounts.

In another variation, represented here (b), the hands are joined to twin hoops united at the base, also known as 'gimmel' from the Latin *gemellus* meaning 'twin'. When closed the hands are clasped and the ring looks like any other with a single hoop, but it is easily opened up to show the twin bands, lying side by side like two lovers. As an additional refinement, the hands have bracelets and diamond rings.

The two high box bezels set with table-cut diamonds in this group (c, d) are supported by elaborate shoulders clearly differentiated from the hoop in the sixteenth-century style. One pair is in the form of scrolls with the Greek key pattern above, flanking a line of lozenges. The other is figurative, in the form of golden-turbaned blackamoors wearing green breeches tied with red sashes. They are reminiscent of the negro pages brought home from tropical parts, who gave an exotic note to banquet scenes painted by Veronese and others.

The carnival ring with bezel in the form of a woman's face, with red lips and rose-diamond eyes peeping mysteriously through her black mask (e), is a souvenir of one of the greatest of all eighteenth-century amusements, the masquerade. The other two rings are simpler, and probably commemorative. One has a silver cluster bezel set with crudely-cut diamonds which may enclose a relic of hair (f), the other, with oblong or square bezel, contains the monogram of the deceased in gold wire under crystal (g). DS
National Museums of Scotland

g

f

a

c

b

d

e

28 *Portrait of a Lady, by Cosmo Alexander, 176[ ].*

This lady, tantalisingly unidentified, wears a formal, low-cut lustrous ivory silk gown trimmed with lace ruffles at the neck and sleeves, with a ladder of ribbon bow-knots on her stomacher. Another ribbon fastens her choker of red beads at the back of the neck. En suite with her necklace is her wheel-like earring.

The aigrette placed over her brow stands out against her neat dark hair, and the bracelet she is clasping round her left wrist matches the one on the right. The bands are composed of red beads strung into several rows with centre pieces of moss agate framed in garnets, a combination which was then the height of fashion. Moss agate, which is a type of chalcedony, is described by the French jeweller Pouget, in his *Traité des Pierres Précieuses* as 'a new discovery of forty years ago which, by a singular trick of nature, has within itself black and sometimes red veins branching out so well that they distinctly resemble bushes, terraces in landscapes, even flowers, animals and sometimes men'. DS

National Trust for Scotland, Haddo House

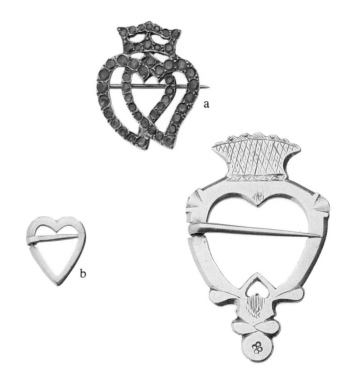

a

b

29 *Selection of heart brooches, early eighteenth century to late nineteenth century.*

Heart-shaped brooches were popular in fourteenth-century France, and there are fifteenth- and sixteenth-century references to them in Scotland, such as the 'hert of gold anamelit [enamelled]' mentioned in the Treasurer's Accounts in 1503. Unfortunately, no surviving Scottish example can safely be dated to much before 1700.

The eighteenth-century brooches were usually made of silver, although gold and base metal examples are known, as are some set with paste stones and garnets (a). Often called 'luckenbooth' brooches, they were said to have been sold in the luckenbooths, or small shops, which clustered round the High Kirk of St Giles in Edinburgh's High Street. As this was the traditional goldsmiths' and jewellers' quarter it is probable that they were sold there, but the name itself cannot be traced before the late nineteenth century. It is more accurate to call them simply 'heart brooches'. Inscriptions on early examples prove that they were love tokens, probably given as engagement or marriage presents. The small

gold example (b) carries the plea 'wrong not the (heart) whos joy thou art', while the silver crowned brooch (c) simply states 'I fancie non but the[e] alon'. The placing of two hearts together, resulting in an 'M' shape, may explain why they have also been known as Queen Mary brooches.

As well as being symbols of love, some brooches were thought to have supernatural powers. In the eighteenth century they were often believed to offer protection against witches: one given to the National Museum in 1893 'was worn on the breast of the chemise by the grandmother of the donor, to prevent the witches from taking away her milk'.

Children, boys as well as girls, had heart brooches pinned inside their petticoats 'for...averting the evil eye and keeping away witches'. Hiding the charm away seems to have made it more powerful.

Towards the end of the eighteenth century the brooches became larger and more complicated in shape. Most now had crowns above the hearts (and twin hearts were common), some with the open type of crowns resembling two birds' heads (d), a design which may have been introduced from Norway, where heart brooches remained popular into the nineteenth century.

By the mid-nineteenth century many brooches were elaborate pieces of jewellery, albeit lacking the naive charm of the older forms, and were being made by established silversmiths in Edinburgh, Glasgow, Inverness and the North East. The means of fastening them on to clothing also changed at this time. The early brooches had very simple pins, similar to those on ring brooches, where the material is pulled through from the back of the brooch and the pin is then pushed through it and locked by the tension of the cloth against the body of the brooch. In the nineteenth century these pins were replaced by the spring pin and catch that is still used today. This was possibly because clothing materials were becoming finer and the tight weave could be damaged by the old style pins.

The change may also represent an alteration in the social status of the brooches. Records and the survival of many early simple heart brooches suggest that they were owned mainly by the ordinary people. Probably they are never shown in portraits because their owners had neither the means nor social position to have their pictures painted. By the late nineteenth century, however, the most elaborate versions would have been fairly expensive and could have been afforded only by the better off. Simpler and less costly brooches did continue to be made, however, and indeed are still popular today. GRD

National Museum of Scotland

c

d

30 *The Deuchar Suite of buckles and earrings, late seventeenth century.*

In 1782 David Deuchar presented the Museum of the Society of Antiquaries with a group of agate-set jewellery which included these buckles, earrings and chain link. The claw settings of the pieces are gilt metal enamelled in green, white and red to represent flowers and leaves. The buckles have jewellers' scratch marks which show they were numbers three and four of a set of at least four. All feature polished agates which could well have originated in Scotland and it is fairly certain that the stones in the longest pair of earrings are from Scurdieness, near Montrose.

Born in 1743, Deuchar had trained as a lapidary under his father, whose business was at Croft-an-Righ near Holyrood in Edinburgh. He later set up on his own as a seal-cutter, engraver and lapidary. His interest in antiquities and history led him to become one of the founding members of the Society, which was established in 1780 by the Earl of Buchan. He is perhaps best known as the person who encouraged the young Henry Raeburn to quit his apprenticeship as a goldsmith and concentrate on portrait painting.

It was originally thought that Deuchar might have made the agate group and presented it to the Museum as a contemporary example of his work. The style is, however, much earlier, and similar pieces in the Museum of London have been dated to the late seventeenth century. It is much more likely that Deuchar acquired the items as unusual specimens, to add to his well-known collection of gems and semi-precious stones. They are therefore some of the earliest examples of pebble-set jewellery in Scotland. GRD

National Museums of Scotland

31 *Anna Bruce of Arnot, by Allan Ramsay, about 1766-7.*

In the mid-eighteenth century, female costume became increasingly elaborate and fancy trimmings such as these left little place for jewellery. The gem-set enamelled brooches of a hundred years earlier would have been completely unsuited to the styles of the 1760s and 70s, earrings had gone out of fashion in portraits and even necklaces had given way to neckbands and ruffs. Pearls did retain their popularity, but not as long necklaces: they would have become too easily entangled with the flowers and the bows on the bodice. Some sitters do appear with a single string of pearls emerging under one arm to be looped up under the breast knot, but the general effect is at best artificial and at worst uncomfortable. Soon, they were abandoned in favour of pearl chokers of one, two, three or even more strands.

All these styles feature in the portraits of Allan Ramsay, who painted this picture of Anna, daughter of Sir John Bruce of Arnot and wife of Thomas Williamson Bruce. She probably sat to him in October 1766 or

1767 when he was in Edinburgh, and her portrait is very reminiscent of one he painted at about the same time of Anne Broun of Colstoun. The pose is similar, both ladies wear the very same fichus but Anna's hair is drawn up into a little bun on top of her head and the length of her neck is emphasised by a delicate single string of pearls worn astonishingly high, while Anne's chin rests on the bows of her deep, satin neckband. RKM
National Gallery of Scotland

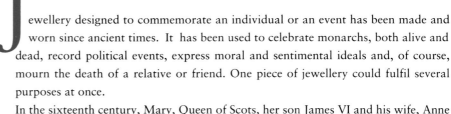

III
COMMEMORATIVE AND MEMORIAL JEWELLERY

J ewellery designed to commemorate an individual or an event has been made and worn since ancient times. It has been used to celebrate monarchs, both alive and dead, record political events, express moral and sentimental ideals and, of course, mourn the death of a relative or friend. One piece of jewellery could fulfil several purposes at once.

In the sixteenth century, Mary, Queen of Scots, her son James VI and his wife, Anne of Denmark frequently gave pieces with their own image or cipher to supporters and followers – a well-established method of encouraging loyalty to the crown. A generation later, the political upheavals of the Civil War and the execution of King Charles I provided ample scope for the jeweller to exercise his skill on politically significant pieces. These not only immortalised the dead king but acted as political propaganda in the Royalist Cause. Some rings, containing miniatures of Charles I, were apparently presented to supporters of the exiled monarchy by Henrietta Maria, his Queen, in appreciation of financial support for the Cause. They acted as a form of security for the loan of cash, to be redeemed after the Restoration on production of the ring.

Given the dangers of the times, most Royalist jewellery could not be worn openly, unless the wearer was out of reach of the Parliamentarians, as Sir William Davidson (34) was when he met Charles II during his exile in Holland. After the Restoration, however, it was diplomatically desirable to have and wear pieces of jewellery associated with either Charles.

After the deposition of James VII and II in 1688, there appeared a vast array of rings, pendant miniatures, medals, cameos, slides and lockets associated with the lost cause of the Jacobites. A large proportion of what is now known as 'Jacobite' jewellery probably originated in the early part of the nineteenth century with the Romantic revival of interest in the movement, but there is still a considerable amount of genuine eighteenth-century jewellery associated with the main figures of the period. Like the earlier Royalist jewellery, there was often little scope for an open display of

detail of 34 Sir William Davidson

44

Jacobite sympathies. Indeed, a good deal of the jewellery of this Cause is secretive and conceals its true meaning. In some cases, however, there could be little doubt as to political allegiance. The 5th Duke of Perth (37) made no secret of his loyalties. Nor could there be any doubting the message conveyed in such pieces as the 'Four Peers' ring, which not only commemorates and mourns the executions of Lords Balmerino, Derwentwater, Kilmarnock and Lovat for their part in the '45, but has the initials of seventeen other Jacobite 'martyrs' who shared their fate.

Memento Mori jewellery, meaning 'remember you must die', was not produced in remembrance of any specific individual. It was an abstract general warning of the impermanence of life and an injunction to make good use of one's time on earth. This view is succinctly expressed in a seventeenth-century book called *Thoughts on Holy Dying,* which told the reader, 'It is a great art to die well and to be learnt by men in health'. Symbols used to remind people of their impending death included coffins, skeletons and, especially, death's heads.

Personal mourning jewellery existed alongside Memento Mori jewellery from the seventeenth century, when it became popular to wear rings, lockets and brooches in remembrance of a departed friend or relative. With the increasing formalisation and complexity of mourning customs, culminating in the rigid social code of late Victorian mourning, the etiquette of wearing the appropriate jewellery became equally elaborate. There were several stages to formal mourning, from the deepest 'First Mourning', through 'Second' and 'Ordinary Mourning' to 'Half Mourning'. The amount of time people spent in each stage varied over the years and according to the closeness of the relative who was being mourned. In the late nineteenth century, a woman would mourn for a total of two and a half years for a dead husband, while he needed to grieve for only three months. In the very deepest mourning, a woman was not permitted to wear any jewellery, but gradually she moved on to matt black jewellery and, later, to appropriate gemstones. Jet was ideal for the purpose, as its surface could be either polished or left dull (41).

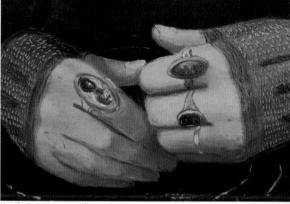

detail of 39 Margaret Whyte

The use of human hair in commemorative jewellery was common for more than three centuries, and it could signify either love or mourning. Much of the early Charles I commemorative jewellery supposedly contained locks of the Martyr King's hair. It is, perhaps, significant that when his coffin was opened in 1813 during the construction of George III's tomb at Windsor Castle, the hair at the back of his head was found to have been cut exceptionally short.

By the nineteenth century, hair of the deceased figured prominently in the full range of mourning jewellery which had become fashionable and could be incorporated in rings (39, 40), lockets or bracelets.

It was also used as a keepsake of a living friend, a practice which found particular favour in the Romantic period. During his courtship of Charlotte Carpenter, Sir Walter Scott sent her a miniature of himself and received in return a lock of her hair to be braided into a ring. She also sent another ringlet to London to be made into 'something mysterious' for him, commenting, 'I have had almost all my hair cut off'. Hair-working was now one of the necessary social accomplishments of a young lady. Design books and instruction manuals and kits were widely advertised and some quite complex pieces were produced by amateurs. The popularity of this type of jewellery dwindled with the coming of the twentieth century, however, and the fading of Victorian sentimentality.

GEORGE R DALGLEISH

32 *Janet Scott, wife of Sir Thomas Kerr of Ferniehirst, by an unknown artist, 1593.*
Janet, the eldest sister of Sir Walter Scott of Buccleuch, married Sir Thomas Kerr in 1569. He was a widower with five children under the age of seven, and together they had three more sons and a daughter. A Roman Catholic and a devoted supporter of Mary, Queen of Scots, Sir Thomas spent long periods in exile, leaving Janet to bring up the family and run his estates. He died at Aberdeen in 1586. This portrait was painted seven years later.

Because of the interval of time, Janet is not in First Mourning, which would have required plain black clothes with no ornamentation. The effect is undeniably sombre, of course, but her widow's peak, with veil wired-out to avoid her ruff, is worn over a gem-set hood of the kind seen in the picture of Agnes, Countess of Argyll (6) and there are vertical lines of decoration on her exaggerated padded sleeves and her deep, pointed bodice.

She also wears a profusion of pearls. A single pearl drop is pinned to her hair beside her left temple and in her left ear she has another pear-shaped pearl. A magnificent double rope of pearls round her neck reaches to her waist, and the point of her bodice is edged with multiple strings of pearls caught together at intervals and terminating in large, pendant pearls. Round each wrist is a double string of pearls.

Visible near her waist is a miniature case, presumably containing a little picture of Sir Thomas. Because she is in mourning, its surface is dull and dark instead of being enamelled and gem-set like Lady Argyll's (6) or Lady Anne Livingston's (10, 11). It too, has its pendant pearl and it is worn from a black ribbon.

The only coloured gem-stones to be seen are in the rings on Janet's left hand. On her other hand is a black keeper, guarding the diamond ring which would be her wedding ring, worn in the Roman Catholic position on the fourth finger of the right hand. RKM

The Duke of Buccleuch and Queensberry KT

b

33 *Selection of Charles II commemorative jewellery, about 1650 to 1685.*

After the execution of his father in 1649, the young Charles became the focus of the Royalist Cause. He was crowned in Scotland in 1651, but after an unsuccessful military campaign which ended in defeat by the Cromwellians at the battles of Dunbar and Worcester, Charles was forced to flee to Holland.

It was not until after the death of Cromwell that he was finally restored to the throne. During his period in exile, his cause was kept alive among his supporters by the circulation of appropriate miniatures, rings and medals. The fine enamelled pendant shows the King with a long ringleted wig and a thin moustache (a). The reverse has a depiction of the crown and sceptre on a blue ground with the motto 'Dieu et mon droit', undoubtedly a reference to the legality of his kingship.

Even after the Restoration, commemorative jewellery circulated. The unusual pendant (b) has a portrait of Charles which seems to be a likeness of him later in life, after he had removed his moustache. Set under a crystal, the central part of the pendant is identical in construction to the memorial slides which were popular at this time (36). It has been mounted in a contemporary gold setting and embellished with table-cut diamonds.   GRD

National Museums of Scotland

a

34 *Sir William Davidson with his son, Charles, attributed to Simon Luttichuys, 1666.*
Clad in sober black, the prosperous cloth merchant Sir William Davidson sits in his handsome chair, fingering his silver watch, while his small son Charles stands at his knee. This picture was painted in the Low Countries, where Sir William was Conservator of the Scottish Staple at Veere and agent of Charles II. His connection with the King was close. They must have met during Charles's exile in Holland and when Sir William's third Dutch wife gave birth to a son in 1661, His Majesty agreed to be godfather.

He did not attend the Amsterdam baptism in person, of course, but he sent Johan Maurice of Nassau to act as his proxy. The Davidson family naturally valued this evidence of royal favour. In the picture the little boy proudly holds up a medallion of his godfather, set with diamonds. It is suspended from a diaphanous blue ribbon round his neck. At his waist is a gold medal which also bears the King's well-known features. It had been struck in 1660 to commemorate Charles II's departure from the Dutch port of Scheveningen, en route for London and his rightful throne. The medal probably hangs from the gold chain seen just below the child's collar: the blue and white ribbons immediately above the medal are trimmings on his black gown.

An inscription on the back of the picture gives the date as 1666. In that year little Charles died. Watches are often included in paintings as reminders of the passage of time and man's mortality. An x-ray examination of the portrait showed that the figure of the child was added later, by a different artist. Presumably this alteration was made after the boy's death, to commemorate his brief life and to emphasise his connection with his famous namesake.   RKM

Scottish National Portrait Gallery

35 Margaret Fraser, Lady Haldane, by an unknown artist, 1666.

Margaret was the daughter of Simon Fraser, 6th Lord Lovat and in 1617 it was arranged that she should marry Sir Robert Arbuthnott of Arbuthnott. When he died in 1633 she was left with four sons and three daughters. Sir John Haldane of Gleneagles was a widower with one small son and three young daughters so it seemed appropriate that they should marry the following year. They completed their large joint family by having two more sons. Sir John was a fervent Covenanter and in 1650 both he and Margaret's son Alexander were with Cromwell's army at Dunbar. Alexander was killed and Sir John was never seen again: presumably he too had perished, although there were rumours that he had been taken prisoner.

Margaret did not marry again but she must have accepted that he was dead, for she wore mourning when she sat for her portrait fourteen years later. Like Lady Kerr (32) a long time had elapsed since her bereavement and so she was able to wear jewellery with her widow's weeds. She is not shown with ropes of pearls, however. Instead, the strings of beads round her neck and wrists are made either of jet or black glass; they are not gemstones.

Pinned to the centre of her cape-like collar is a fine breast jewel composed of lines of square-cut stones, possibly black garnets. There may be pearls in the two rectangular areas immediately above the horizontal crescent. The table-cutting of the stones and the design incorporating the three pendant pearls suggests that this is rather an old-fashioned jewel, dating from the late sixteenth or early seventeenth century rather than from the 1660s.

Similarly, the large ring with square-cut stone on the small finger of her right hand seems to come from an earlier period, but the diamond in the quatrefoil setting on her other hand has a more modern appearance. RKM

The Viscount of Arbuthnott

36 *Selection of memorial slides and pendants, about 1660 to 1714*

From the reign of Charles II to that of Queen Anne it was very fashionable to wear this type of ornament, usually on a velvet ribbon, either round the neck or on the wrist. Most surviving examples are a form of mourning jewellery, commemorating both royalty and private individuals. Some, however, do appear to have been exchanged as marriage or betrothal gifts.

Characteristically, they are made up of a gold setting with a large table- or fancy-cut rock crystal covering either a monogram in gold wire or a miniature. Their backs are often enamelled with floral designs on white, although plain gold backs with inscriptions also occur. Many have borders of diamonds, pearls and garnets, into which the central crystal mount is fixed.

The plain gold pendant shown here (a) contains a verse lamenting the death of William II and III, while a slide (b) has a miniature of his wife Mary II, shown with a skull as a symbol of mortality. She died before him in 1694 and, on his death in 1702, a slide commemorating her was found on a ribbon tied round his arm. William's successor Queen Anne is also represented, along with her husband Prince George of Denmark (c). The other pair of slides (d) with intricately worked initials and coronets supported by cupids probably commemorates a marriage.

The rarest and most unusual example of this type of jewellery is the exquisite necklace of thirty-one crystal-covered 'medallions'. All contain gold wire initials, and they are also engraved on their backs. Unfortunately it is not known to whom these initials refer, but it is unlikely that they are all members of the same family.   GRD

National Museums of Scotland

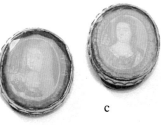

c

a

b

d

37 *John Drummond, 5th titular Duke of Perth, by John Alexander, 1735.*

This portrait depicts the 5th Jacobite Duke of Perth in a soldier's armour, although he seems to have been one of the few members of his family who was not 'out' during either the 1715 or 1745 Risings. There can be no doubt about his political allegiance, however. His military fur cape is fastened at the shoulder with a very fine gold mounted cameo of the Old Pretender, King James VIII and III to the Jacobites.

The image of James is similar to that which appears on a series of medals produced in the early years of the eighteenth century and it may be based on an original by the medallist Norbert Roettier. It also reflects the artist John Alexander's own political leanings. In his early years he painted for the Jacobite court in Rome, before returning to Edinburgh in 1720. He was 'out' in the '45, but seems to have escaped any punishment and was back at work in 1748.

The sitter was a younger son of James, 4th Earl and 1st titular Duke of Perth. The dukedom had been created by James VII and II after Perth had been exiled and forfeited by King William for his opposition to him, therefore the title existed only in the eyes of Jacobite supporters. Both his brother and his nephews held the title before him, and had been heavily involved in the abortive attempts to restore the exiled Stewarts. James, the 3rd Duke, had been Bonnie Prince Charlie's lieutenant-general throughout the '45, commanding the left wing at Culloden.

The 5th Duke succeeded to the title in 1747, after the death of his nephew. Born in 1679, he had been educated in France at the Scots College at Douai. He spent the early part of his life abroad, living at the courts of France and Spain, before returning to Scotland, where this picture was probably painted. GRD

Mrs Flora Maxwell Stuart

c

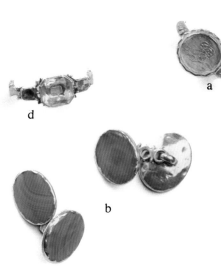

a

d

b

38a *Selection of jewellery associated with the Jacobite Risings, 1688-1747.*

The 'Jacobite Century', initiated by King James VII and II's flight from London in 1688, produced a vast range of mementos of important figures on both sides of the political divide, for the houses of Orange and Hanover were equally eager to win the propaganda war. A great deal of commemorative jewellery of one kind or another has survived to this day, simply because it was associated with the 'heroes' of the period, much of it acquiring the status of relics of the often confused current political and moral ideologies.

When James VII escaped from London on the night of 10 December 1688, he was helped by Sir Peter Halkett of Pitfirrane, a loyal courtier whom he rewarded with a gold enamelled ring set with the royal monogram under crystal (a).

The battle of Prestonpans in 1745 was the

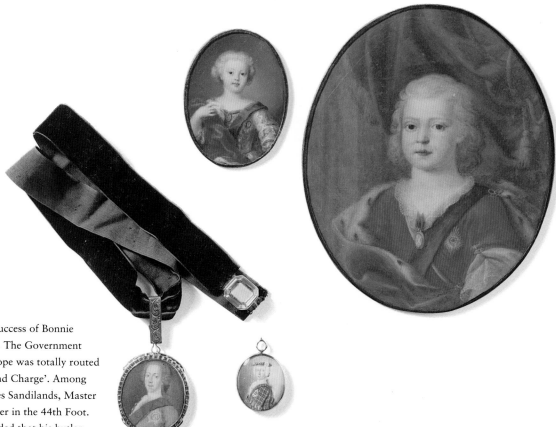

height of the military success of Bonnie Prince Charlie's Rising. The Government army under General Cope was totally routed by the famous 'Highland Charge'. Among the casualties was James Sandilands, Master of Torphichen, an officer in the 44th Foot. He was so badly wounded that his butler, who was also at the battle, thought he was dead and removed his silver and agate sleeve links (b). The Master did recover, however, only to die four years later; it is not recorded whether he had repossessed his sleeve links.

One of the most famous figures linked with Bonnie Prince Charlie was undoubtedly Flora MacDonald, who helped him escape from Hanoverian soldiers. A large number of relics has come to be associated with her, but the gold ring set with crystal (c) has a better claim than most to be truly hers. The gold and enamelled hoop has a typical Jacobite motto and motifs.

A less affectionately regarded figure of the '45 was Simon Fraser, Lord Lovat. A crafty man, he eventually sided with the Prince but was unable to save himself from the ruin that befell many Jacobites after the debacle of Culloden. He died under the headsman's axe on 9 April 1747, and is commemorated by the gold and enamelled ring, set with his hair under a crystal (d). GRD
National Museums of Scotland

38b *Miniatures of Prince Charles Edward Stewart.*

Stewart supporters at the exiled Jacobite court in Rome waged a propaganda war against the Hanoverians, and in so doing they commissioned and distributed large numbers of medals, mementos and miniatures. These were given to friends to encourage loyalty and simply to keep the images of the exiled royal family uppermost in their minds. Jacobitism was revitalised by the birth of Prince Charles Edward Stewart, who was regarded by his supporters as the true-born Prince of Wales and the rightful heir to the thrones of Great Britain. Throughout his life, Charles was painted by some of the best court painters in Europe. Frequently these portraits were copied and imitated by lesser artists, thereby creating a wealth of images of the Prince, ranging in quality from excellent to barely recognisable. Large numbers of miniatures in particular circulated among Jacobite supporters and

many were incorporated into pendants and other items of jewellery.

The first two above, showing Charles at about eighteen months and five years, are fine examples, and may have been the work of the Italian painter Antonio David, who was appointed to the Jacobite court in 1718, and is recorded as having painted miniatures of Charles in 1723. They were in the collection of Sir John Hynde Cotton, leader of the English Jacobite faction in Parliament, and may have been given by Charles's father, James VIII, as a means of keeping his supporters aware of the progress of his children.

The gold pendant has a rather poor quality image, loosely based on the engraving of the Prince by the Scottish artist Robert Strange. The other miniature is also based on Strange's work and was originally incorporated in a wrist clasp, surrounded with garnets, later converted to a pendant. GRD
National Museums of Scotland

39 *Margaret Whyte, by Taverner Knott, from an original painting of about 1775.*
Margaret Whyte was the wife of James Hogue, minister of the Secession Church in Kelso. She was originally painted by an unknown artist, probably working in the Borders, and then this copy was made by Knott. A portraitist also known for his chalk drawings, he was in Edinburgh in the early 1840s and then exhibited from a Glasgow address.

Clad in her smart, beribboned cap and fringed shawl, with mittens on her hands, Mrs Hogue proudly displays a fine selection of mourning rings. These are mainly rings with the oval-shaped bezels which were currently in fashion. However, the giving and wearing of mourning rings was an ancient practice, not confined to the end of the eighteenth century.

In the Middle Ages it was common to give away the rings of the deceased to his friends or relatives. This soon developed into the custom of providing a number of specially bought rings to be donated to mourners at the funeral. Wills frequently stipulated how many and the prices to be paid. By the eighteenth century, special mourning rings had been developed. They were engraved or decorated in enamel, with the name and dates of the deceased, for presentation to the male mourners, who in turn gave them to their wives.

This practice grew in scale, especially with the increasingly complex set of rules which governed Victorian mourning customs, and from the last quarter of the eighteenth century mourning rings were being virtually mass-produced by jewellers in London, Birmingham and Edinburgh to meet the heavy demand. By the end of the nineteenth century, however, the custom had ceased to be fashionable with the aristocracy, although it continued to be extremely popular with the middle class. GRD
J D F Miller Esq

40 *Selection of mourning rings, 1748 to 1831.*
This group shows the changing design of mourning rings over an eighty year period. The earliest example, set with a garnet and six rose-cut diamonds, has an enamelled hoop very similar in style to Jacobite commemorative rings of the time (38a). It records the death of C Crawford on 18 June 1748.

As the eighteenth century wore on, the fashion was for oval or vesica shaped bezels, with appropriate symbols of mourning, such as the weeping willow, a sepulchral urn and a grieving woman, set under glass. The inscription commemorating the deceased was picked out in black and white enamel round the bezel or, later, was engraved on the back. Different styles were popular at the same time, and indeed could be distributed for the same funeral. The plain gold and enamel hoop ring and the one with the oval enamelled bezel above (a, b) were both made to commemorate the death of Charles Steuart on 27 November 1797. He was Surveyor General of Customs in British North America, and died at the age of seventy-two. The second ring shows evidence of having been mass-produced, for the personalised bezel has been incorporated into a standard hoop. As we have seen above (39), large numbers of rings were often distributed at funerals.

Not surprisingly, the hair of the deceased was frequently preserved in a mourning ring, either under a glass bezel, or in a compartment within the hoop, as in the ring above (c) which also displays the contemporary fashion for heavy cast floral decoration. Jet, too, was used in later rings, and could be included with locks of hair. Another ring (d) records 'SJ/died 29th May/1831'. GRD
National Museums of Scotland

41 *Selection of jet jewellery, second half of the nineteenth century.*

One of the finest suites of jet jewellery in existence in Scotland was worn in Edinburgh by Mrs Craig, mother of the Selkirkshire historian, Thomas Craig Brown, in the second half of the nineteenth century. The complete set consists of a massive pendant chain, three pairs of bracelets, a delicate drop necklace with a pendant cross, a brooch, a hair comb and a faceted necklace. Jet is a very compact variety of lignite or coal, formed by the action of heat and pressure on ancient deposits of driftwood. It has been used to fashion jewellery and ornaments from prehistory onwards, its principal source in Britain since Roman times being the shale beds of the Yorkshire coast near Whitby. Its hard, dense nature makes it extremely effective for carving, faceting, engraving and polishing. This versatility and of course its colour made it especially popular for mourning jewellery in

the second half of the nineteenth century and by 1870 about 1400 men and boys were employed in the Whitby jet industry. Different finishes were produced for the various stages of mourning, with a dull, matt surface reserved for deepest mourning. Good quality, intricately carved pieces were fragile and therefore expensive. This, combined with a shortage of the best quality Whitby jet after about 1885, led to a variety of substitutes and imitations becoming more popular. These included French jet (a type of hard, black glass), Vauxhall glass (black glass, originally made at the Vauxhall glassworks in London), vulcanite (an early form of plastic made from rubber which could be moulded) and bog oak. GRD
National Museums of Scotland

42 *Princess Marie of Baden, Duchess of Hamilton, by James Rannie Swinton, about 1859.*

Princess Marie was the daughter of the Grand Duke Charles Louis Frederick of Baden, and Stephanie, niece of Napoleon I. In 1843, she married the Marquess of Douglas, future 11th Duke of Hamilton. Seated in front of a Highland landscape, she wears an ivory silk gown trimmed with a red and white ribbon bow-knot and sash beneath a Spanish-style black silk gauze shawl. Her hair is severely dressed with a plait drawn across the crown.

On her marriage, her husband and her mother bought a diamond garland for her hair and a turquoise and diamond stomacher brooch from the best Parisian maker, Fossin, of 78 rue de Richelieu. The jewels shown here, however, are not indicative of her rank and wealth. She has small pearls in her ears and a plain gold band on her finger: presumably hidden under her hand, a locket hangs from the thin gold neckchain.

Her wrists are loaded with bracelets. On the right is a thick gold bangle highlighted with enamel and diamonds: perhaps a snake, emblem of eternity. The larger of the two bracelets on the left wrist has a centrepiece set with a miniature of a boy, almost certainly her son, the future 12th Duke of Hamilton, born in 1845. Next to it is a heavy chain hung with charms, seals, and heart-shaped and round lockets containing mementos of family and friends. This emphasis on sentiment rather than wealth is typical of the spirit of the Romantic period. DS

National Trust for Scotland,
Brodick Castle

43 *Pair of gold bracelet clasps set with silhouettes by John Miers, about 1788.*

The navette-shaped clasps with bright-cut borders were worn on the wrists, attached to six rows of seed pearls or beads. They contain portrait silhouettes on ivory of John, 4th Duke of Atholl and his wife Jane Cathcart, by John Miers (1758-1821) the leading exponent of such silhouettes, which were in fashion from the 1770s. Copies could easily be made from the original likeness and another silhouette of the Duchess, in a private collection, has a label on the back, advertising 'Perfect Likenesses in Miniature Profile taken by J. MIERS, LEEDS, and reduced on a plan entirely new which preserves the most exact Symmetry and animated expression of the Features much Superior to any other method. Time of sitting one Minute. N.B. He keeps the original Shades, and can supply those he has once taken with any number of Copies. Those who have shades by them may have them reduced to any Size and dressed in the Present Taste'. Miers settled in Edinburgh from 1786-8 and then moved to London in 1789, taking premises in the Strand. He died in 1821. Duchess Jane, daughter of the 9th Lord Cathcart, was born in 1754, and married in 1774. An idyllic portrait by David Allan depicts her out of doors with her husband and three children, enjoying the Highland scenery. The happy atmosphere at Blair Castle was also observed by Robert Burns, who spent two days there in 1787: 'I shall never forget the fine family piece I saw at Blair: the amiable, the truly noble Duchess, with her smiling little seraph on her lap, at the head of the table. The lovely olive plants as the Hebrew bard finely says, round the happy Mother...I wish I had the powers of Guido to do them justice! My Lord Duke's hospitality markedly kind indeed...'

Much afflicted by the death of her young brother, Charles Cathcart, in 1788, followed by the death of her baby, Frederick, the Duchess fell ill and died in 1790. DS

From His Grace the Duke of Atholl's
Collection at Blair Castle, Perthshire

IV

HIGHLAND JEWELLERY

It is perhaps misleading to distinguish 'Highland Jewellery' as somehow separate from developments in the rest of Scotland, especially as recent research has tended to suggest that the cultural, social and economic differences between the Highlands and the Lowlands are perhaps more illusory than real. Be that as it may, a fine corpus of early jewellery and personal accoutrements with a Highland provenance, and decorated in what has become known as a West Highland style, undoubtedly exists. What is both fascinating and perplexing is how rarely such jewellery appears in portraiture or in Gaelic literature. This is thrown into sharp focus when one realises how important dress and personal adornment were to the Highlanders in their scale of cultural values. Writing in the late eighteenth century, David Stewart of Garth, an accurate chronicler of Highland society, noted that Highlanders would willingly do without food and shelter in order to 'procure arms and habiliments which would set off to advantage a person unbent and unsubdued by conscious inferiority'. Yet although there are many references in Gaelic poetry and prose which describe in detail their fine clothing, weapons and accoutrements, specific mentions of items of jewellery are conspicuously absent. Similarly, John Michael Wright's handsome portrait of Sir Mungo Murray captures the splendour of his sitter's costume, but his only jewellery is a very discreet brooch at his throat (44).

It is paradoxical therefore that some of the most impressive examples of sixteenth-century jewellery in Scotland have Highland provenances. These are the massive and magnificent 'reliquary' brooches associated with the families which owned the lands of Lorne, Lossit/Ugadale, Lochbuie, Glenlyon and Ballochyle (45). Most are set with charmstone crystals, which were objects of reverence and superstitious awe, and the silver settings may have been of subsidiary importance.

A later inscription on the Lochbuie Brooch maintains that it was made of native Mull silver about 1500. The Ballochyle Brooch has an unknown maker's mark which suggests that it was probably made by an established burgh silversmith about 1600. Whether or not all or any were made in the Highlands, they do seem to have their

detail of 44 Sir Mungo Murray

origins in the earlier, simple form of ring brooch which was common in many parts of Europe in the medieval period.

This tradition continued in the Highlands long after it had died out elsewhere, and in the seventeenth and eighteenth centuries large flat ring brooches became the dominant form of jewellery (47). An old story preserved in a seventeenth-century manuscript confirms that they were worn by women to fasten their plaids or shawls. It relates that Duncan, ancestor of the Robertsons of Struan and a great reiver, had incurred the anger of King Robert II. 'Duncan put on a woman's habit, and a great brooch at his breast, alleging that he himself was Duncan's mother and so went to Stirling to intercede for Duncan'. This piece of deception was taken in good part by the King, and Duncan went on to found the fortunes of the Robertsons.

The earliest brooches were brass, formed from a single ingot, beaten flat into a ring with a notched join where the pin was slipped in. The surfaces were deeply engraved and divided into panels by four or six circles, which were filled with interlace and grotesque animals. This type of decoration occurred on other Highland accoutrements, notably the circular shields, or targes, and on powder horns and dirks. By the eighteenth century the brooches were being made of silver, often inlaid with niello, a black silver sulphide compound, with an anchor design. Although still Highland in character, the best of these were from the North East and occasionally from silversmiths in Glasgow and Edinburgh. Many of these brooches have survived, but the only known portrait of someone wearing one is that of the Hen Wife of the Laird of Grant (46).

The defeat of the Jacobite forces of Prince Charles Edward Stewart at Culloden in 1746 led to the suppression of Highland dress and its associated weapons and adornments. The Highland regiments of the government army, raised to combat the Jacobite threat and then to fight Britain's American and Continental wars, were the only Scots legally allowed to wear tartan after the Disarming Act of 1746. They helped to preserve the concept and prestige of Highland costume, so that when the Scottish Romantics looked for a model for a 'national' costume they found it in the army.

Proscription was not entirely successful and by the 1780s, with the encouragement of influential individuals and groups like the Highland Society of London, Highland dress had become not only tolerated but fashionable (50). In the nineteenth century 'dress' and 'uniform' became 'national costume', and the weapons which had been a functional part of the Highlanders' outfit became fashion accessories.

Although traditional types were used, the decorative inspiration was British and from the South – a development which caused distaste among some Scots. A profusion of thistles, often in association with roses and shamrocks, and St Andrew crosses, as well as standard decorative motifs appeared on powder horns, swords, sword belts and dirks (49). Men now also wore brooches, pinned to the plaid where it was brought up to the shoulder. These 'plaid brooches' were inspired by the traditional ring brooches, but had lost their original use and cultural significance.

Undoubtedly, the pinnacle of this process of popularisation of Highland costume and ornament was reached with King George IV's visit to Edinburgh in August 1822. At his first levée, held in Holyroodhouse, the King appeared in full Highland garb. His Highland accoutrements had been supplied by George Hunter of Tokenhouse Yard, London and Edinburgh. They consisted of gem-set shoe rosettes, 'a goatskin

detail of 46 Laird of Grant's Hen Wife

detail of 48 Colonel James Moray

Highland purse with massive gold spring top' and nine tassels of gold-bullion, a fine gold ornament for his bonnet set with a miniature Royal Scottish crown of diamonds, pearls, rubies and emeralds 'supported on a wreath of chased gold Thistles surrounding a sea green emerald, large size', a gold-mounted powder horn suspended from a massive gold chain, a dirk inlaid with gold in a gold-mounted red velvet scabbard and a basket-hilted sword. His costume was little more fanciful than that of his Scottish hosts. This style of 'Highland Garb' continued in fashion well into the middle of the century and Colonel James Moray's portrait of 1838 (48, 49) depicts him almost as fully equipped as the King.

By the second half of the nineteenth century a new phase in the development of 'Highland' jewellery begins to manifest itself, this time influenced by the archaeological scholarship at the root of the 'Celtic Revival'. Publication of accurate representations of Celtic brooches, like the superb Hunterston Brooch, and other early Highland accoutrements and jewellery provided accurate models for the jewellers of this later 'Revival'.

Scottish jewellery exhibited by trade firms such as Rettie of Aberdeen (1851 and 1862), Marshall & Sons of Edinburgh (1851 and 1878), Muirhead of Glasgow (1862) and Mackay Cunningham of Edinburgh (1872), was regarded as part of the wider Celtic archaeological heritage and much of the work produced in the east of Scotland, the real heartland of the 'Celtic Revival' movement, shows striking links with the craftsmen of Ireland. The enamel work of the magnificent dirk scabbard by William Marshall of Edinburgh, 1884-5, (52) seems to be based on early Irish examples rather than on Scottish inspiration.

The vogue for 'Revival' jewellery and other metalwork was to continue in Scotland until the end of the nineteenth century.   GEORGE R DALGLEISH & CHARLOTTE GERE

44 *Sir Mungo Murray, by John Michael Wright, about 1683.*

For many years this portrait intrigued costume and jewellery historians, for its identity was something of a mystery. It shows a youth of the 1680s, in full Highland dress. He is evidently out deerhunting, for his servant carries a longbow and he himself is equipped with flintlock sporting gun, scroll-butt pistol, powder horn and two brass flasks of shot. His costume, however, is that of no ordinary Highlander. He wears the traditional belted plaid but his elegant, feather-trimmed bonnet, his slashed gold doublet, his voluminous lace-trimmed shirt and his extravagant golden garters are more suited to an audience at court than a day on the hills.

Because of the sophistication of his outfit, there was at one time a great deal of debate about his identity. The painting was known as 'The Highland Chief' and its artist was recognised as being John Michael Wright, but some experts harboured dark suspicions that the sitter was really an actor in stage costume. Surely, they argued, a genuine Highlander would have appeared in brightly-coloured tartan, encrusted with 'cairngorm' brooches, silver-mounted pistols, an elaborate sporran and a set of fancy buttons. This youth's only jewellery is a modest oval brooch at the neck of his shirt.

These doubts were finally dispelled in 1988, when Jane Fenlon published the result of her researches. The inventories of the Dukes of Ormonde record that the elegant youth was indeed a perfectly authentic Highland aristocrat: Sir Mungo Murray, younger son of the 2nd Earl of Atholl. The picture was painted about 1683, when he was fifteen, probably during his stay with the Ormonde family in Ireland. This magnificent portrait therefore provides a unique record of authentic Highland dress, jewellery and accoutrements of the late seventeenth century and is in dramatic contrast to the often fanciful resplendence of Victorian imagery. RKM

Scottish National Portrait Gallery

45 *The Ballochyle Brooch, about 1600.*
Of silver gilt, set with a hemisphere of rock crystal, the brooch is inscribed with a confused talismanic motto 'De Serve and Haif the Hevin Babaif', the initials 'MC' and shields with the Campbell and MacIver family arms. It was an heirloom and charm of the MacIvor-Campbell family of Ballochyle in Cowal, Argyllshire and it was supposed to have great healing powers, as well as being proof against witchcraft.
It is perhaps the last in the line of great Scottish medieval brooches, worn by their owners as symbols of authority and prestige; but it also anticipates several developments in the seventeenth and eighteenth centuries. It is decorated with a mixture of Renaissance and later motifs which suggest that it was made about 1600.
On the back is a maker's mark 'AS' (or 'SV'), stamped twice, along with an 'assay scrape', made when metal was taken from it to test its quality. This evidence all

suggests that the brooch was made by an established goldsmith, probably working in a town, who was aware of the laws regulating the testing and marking of gold and silver and was complying with them. Unfortunately, the maker has not yet been identified. GRD

National Museums of Scotland

The HEN WIFE
Castle GRANT
A, D, 1706

46 *Nic Ciarain, the Hen Wife of Castle Grant, by Richard Waitt, about 1726.*

Richard Waitt painted a remarkable series of portraits of the retainers of the Lairds of Grant, between 1713 and 1726. Alexander Grant, and after him his son Sir James, still maintained a traditional Gaelic court at their home at Castle Grant on Speyside, where they were attended by their kinsmen, members of the Grant clan, hereditary pipers, poets and warrior champions. The Grant chiefs were unique in employing a painter to record this court life and in so doing they produced the beginnings of a clan portrait gallery.

The picture of the Hen Wife, or *Cailleach nan Cearc*, is particularly important as it depicts one of the ordinary people, an out-of-doors member of the household. Waitt's bill to the Laird, dated October 1726, has the entry 'For old Naikairn her picture ...[25 shillings]'. Naikairn is probably a phonetic attempt at a Gaelic surname – she may have been either the daughter of the son of (Nic) Cairan or of Eachairn. It is an extraordinarily detailed and unidealised image, showing the old woman in the act of taking snuff from a horn 'mull', or snuff box. (The Scots, women as well as men, were renowned for their addiction to snuff – the 'sneeshin'.)

Her dress is equally fascinating: she is shown wearing a 'kertch', a headdress popular in the seventeenth and early eighteenth centuries, and also a 'tonnag', or shawl, fastened with a ring brooch. This is a rare illustration of a sitter wearing what was one of the commonest forms of jewellery in the Highlands. Probably made of brass, the brooch is a relatively small example of its type, possibly because it is used here to fasten the lesser shawl rather than the plaid, the *arisaid*. It is clear from the Hen Wife's portrait that these brooches were fastened by drawing the material of the shawl through from the back, pushing the pin through and then locking it against the brooch by the 'pull' of the cloth. GRD

A Private Collection

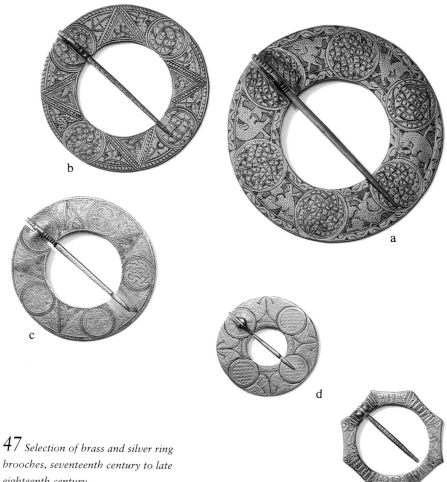

47 *Selection of brass and silver ring brooches, seventeenth century to late eighteenth century.*

Ring brooches were a feature of European dress from the twelfth century but they developed in a specific way in the Scottish Highlands between the sixteenth and eighteenth centuries. The best of the brass brooches date to the late seventeenth or early eighteenth century and are notable for their vigorous engraving of curious animals, foliage and roundels with interlace. They were worn by women only; men fastened their plaids with pins.

Martin Martin, in his description of the Western Isles about 1700, says that the *arisaid*, or womens' plaid, was 'tied before on the breast with a buckle of silver or brass according to the quality of the wearer...[some were] as broad as any pewter plate'. This is an appropriate description for the large brass brooch from Tomintoul, Banffshire (a). Silver brooches became more common about 1700 and the one shown

above (c) illustrates that initially the spirited designs of the earlier brass brooches were continued in silver.

In the eighteenth century the silver brooches were often engraved with initials and dates, showing that they were frequently given as betrothal gifts. The quality of the design began to decline in the second half of the century, becoming very stereotyped with the interlace degenerating into mere hatching. This can be seen on the brooch above (d), which also has the charming inscription 'For nursing Colin Campbell, Mellords [my lord's] fourth son Ap[ril] 1777. Sara Livingston'. Wet-nursing was still a widespread and important practice well into the eighteenth century, with the nurse holding an honoured place in the family. GRD

National Museums of Scotland

48 *Lieutenant Colonel James Moray, by Robert McInnes, 1838.*

This striking and unusually accurate depiction of a laird in full Highland dress was painted only two years before James Moray of Abercairney's death in 1840. Born sixty years earlier, James Moray succeeded his father as 16th Laird of Abercairney in Perthshire. He served in the 15th Hussars before becoming a Lieutenant Colonel of the Perthshire Militia. A considerable 'character', he was renowned locally for his interests in hunting and architecture and he combined these enthusiasms when he added an extravagant set of stables for his horses

and hounds to Abercairney House, built by his father in the popular grand Gothic style. Family tradition maintains that the portrait represents him in the costume he wore for George IV's momentous visit to Scotland in 1822, when Moray, or his brother William, impressed the King with his dancing abilities. It is quite possible that the portrait was done retrospectively. It certainly shows the fullest development of nineteenth-century 'Highland Dress', influenced as it was by revival of traditional Highland forms and borrowings from military uniform. The artist, Robert McInnes, was born in 1801 and began his career as a coach painter

with the Edinburgh coach building firm of Crichton, Gall and Thomson. He exhibited at the Royal Academy in London from 1841, and seems to have lived there for a considerable period. He finally settled in Stirling, where he died in 1886. GRD
A Private Collection

49 *Accoutrements of the Highland Dress of James Moray of Abercairney, about 1822-38.*

A full set of 'Highland' accoutrements was essential for the fashion-conscious patriotic Scottish laird of the first half of the nineteenth century. James Moray's set shows how accurately the painter depicted them (48). They consist of a basket-hilted sword and dirk with gilt metal decorative mounts, set with faceted citrines; an elaborate horse-hair sporran with a gilt metal cantle cast with the Moray coat of arms; black leather waist and sword belts with gilt metal heraldic mounts; a powder horn; a cartridge case; a cap badge incorporating the Moray crest; a steel flintlock pistol and a fine plaid brooch, with a double ring of faceted stones, the crest, motto and coronet of the family. All these items had their origins in the weapons and jewellery of the seventeenth- and eighteenth-century Highlanders, but by the nineteenth century they had been imbued with the Romanticism of the period, resulting in a very stylised effect.

The prolific use of crests, arms and heraldic motifs suggests that Moray had a great pride in his august ancestry. Unfortunately, there are no manufacturers' marks, except on the pistol, made by Daniel Ross, an Edinburgh gun maker who was working between 1815 and 1839. (He became very successful, and presented the city of Edinburgh with the spectacular fountain from the Paris Exhibition, now in Princes Street Gardens.) The vogue for Highland Dress with all the necessary accoutrements meant that a considerable trade in these items grew up, especially in Edinburgh, where several companies specialised in supplying them. GRD
A Private Collection

50 *Selection of accoutrements from the*
Duke of Sussex's Highland outfit, 1801-
1805.

Born in 1773, Prince Augustus Frederick,
Duke of Sussex, was the sixth son of King
George III and younger brother of the Prince
Regent, later George IV. He supported
Catholic Emancipation, abolition of the
slave trade and the reform movement and
his radical political views led to friction with
his father and brother. He did, however,
share his brother's enthusiasm for Scotland
and the growing Romantic view of its
history. This was perhaps fostered by his
secret marriage to Lady Augusta Murray,
daughter of the Earl of Dunmore, in 1793.
He was an early and influential member of
the Highland Society of London, becoming
its President in 1806, 1813 and 1825. The
Society had been founded in 1778,
principally to campaign for the repeal of the
Disarming Act of 1746, which had
forbidden the wearing of Highland dress
after the '45 Rising.
George IV's visit to Scotland in 1822 is often
seen as the beginning of the popular rage for

'tartanry'. This is misleading, as there had
already been a considerable growth of
interest in all things romantically Scottish in
the late eighteenth century. The earliest
pieces in the Sussex accoutrements date to
1801, over twenty years before the Royal
visit, and are important early examples of
the nineteenth-century 'revival' of Highland
dress and ornament.
The sword, made in London in 1805, is a
direct copy of Bonnie Prince Charlie's silver-
hilted sword, captured at Culloden in 1746.
The original sword was also made in
London, in 1740, and had been presented to
Prince Charles by James, 3rd Duke of Perth.
Sussex's brother George owned it in the
early nineteenth century, later giving it to his
friend and courtier, Ranald MacDonald,
chief of Clanranald.
Sussex's two sporrans are equally

fascinating: one is of leopard skin with gilt
mounts, the other of white horsehair with
silver mounts. Both were made in London in
1805, and are set with agates. In the centres
of each are gold, enamelled and diamond-
mounted St Andrew Badges of the Order of
the Thistle. The badges are identical to two
now in the National Museums, which came
from the Clanranald Collection. As most of
the important parts of this set were made
in 1805, it is probable that they were
commissioned by the Duke just before he was
made President of the Highland Society.   GRD
The Scottish Tartans Museum,
Comrie, Perthshire

51 Colonel Alexander Sebastian Leith Hay, by J M Barclay, 1868.

Known to his family as Alick, Colonel Leith Hay was a professional soldier and is depicted here in the uniform of the 93rd Sutherland Highlanders. He joined the army as a boy of seventeen in 1835 and fought with distinction in the Crimean War, where he was with the famous 'Thin Red Line'. He was also at the Canadian rebellion of 1857-9 and the Indian Mutiny, where he led the Highlanders at the Relief of Lucknow. His military exploits earned him, among other honours, a knighthood of the Legion of Honour and the Order of Medjidie, which he is shown wearing, along with a fine silver plaid brooch.

In his earlier years he became an accomplished dancer, and he must have cut a fine figure at a ball in Buckingham Palace where he was asked by Queen Victoria to demonstrate Highland steps to foreign guests. He became Laird of Leith Hall in Aberdeenshire in 1862 and developed a reputation as a rather fiery but kindly figure. The artist, John Maclaren Barclay, was a Perth man who exhibited frequently at the Royal Academies in London and Edinburgh. This portrait was shown at the Royal Scottish Academy in the year it was painted. GRD
National Trust for Scotland, Leith Hall

52 Silver and enamelled dirk and scabbard, mounted with garnets and citrines, with en suite *silver-mounted horsehair sporran, by William Marshall, Edinburgh, 1884-5; silver ring brooch, by Ferguson Brothers, Inverness, about 1860s-70s.*

This dirk and sporran are examples of the 'Celtic Revival' style at its most exuberant. The design of the inset filigree panels showing fantastic beasts was undoubtedly inspired by the discovery of such archaeological treasures as the Hunterston Brooch and the Irish Tara Brooch. The enamelling, and especially the raised studs, also suggest the Irish influence of pieces like the Ardagh Chalice. Several Dublin jewellers and goldsmiths, for example Waterhouse and Company, produced replicas of important Irish Celtic metalwork in the middle of the century. In Scotland, craftsmen drew inspiration from exhibitions like that of the Archaeological Institute held in Edinburgh in 1856. Similarly, accurate drawings of Celtic and Highland metalwork were being published by academics like Joseph Anderson, Keeper of the Museum of Antiquities.

The maker of these exceptional pieces, William Marshall and Company, was an old-established Edinburgh firm, working at 134 Princes Street. A few years after making this dirk they applied to the Museum of Antiquities for permission to produce a replica of the Hunterston Brooch. Despite the fact that they were refused, small-scale replicas by the firm were soon in circulation. The silver ring brooch is based directly on the early Highland brass ring brooches of the seventeenth century (47). Although it does have a working 'old-style' pin, it was actually fixed to a plaid with a new type of spring pin at the back. A large number of replicas or copies of early ring brooches was produced in the later nineteenth and early twentieth century to satisfy the great demand for 'Celtic' ornament. Some were so realistic that unmarked ones can easily be confused with the originals. William and James Ferguson were trading as jewellers and silversmiths in Inverness from about 1860 until at least 1878. GRD
Glasgow Museums and Art Galleries

53 *Plaid brooch of the Chiefs of Clanranald, second half of the nineteenth century.*

This massive pierced silver brooch, set with a central citrine and surrounded by cabochon garnets, shows how elaborate these brooches became. Although they were based on the plain silver and brass ring brooches (47), nineteenth-century taste soon ensured that some of them left the original simplicity far behind. The ring shape combined with popular Scottish semi-precious stones, such as 'cairngorms', to give rise to some spectacular examples. (Although most amber-coloured quartzes are often referred to as 'cairngorms', only a relatively few came from the Scottish mountains and can be truly given that name. The majority originated in South America.) Although the earlier ring brooches were worn by women on the breast, these nineteenth-century examples were placed on a man's shoulder to decorate his plaid. This one belonged to Roderick MacDonald, 20th Chief of Clanranald and was preserved by his descendants 'as a specimen of the fashions in vogue at the time'. It was presented to the National Museum with the other Jacobite and family relics of the Clanranalds by Angus Roderick MacDonald, 23rd Chief. GRD
National Museums of Scotland

54 *James Scott Skinner, by David Waterson, 1912.*

This striking portrait of one of Scotland's most celebrated and prolific fiddle composers shows him wearing two splendid silver plaid brooches. They decorate his fly-plaid, which is loosely draped over his left shoulder, and are probably set with citrines and amethysts. Both date to the end of the nineteenth century but, like a lot of Scottish jewellery of that period, they are based on much earlier forms. He also has a chain draped across his chest to hold his decorative powder horn, an important part of Highland dress.

Scott Skinner was born at Banchory in 1843, and during his long life produced over six hundred published fiddle tunes, many of which remain popular favourites today. According to the artist's widow, the picture shows Skinner as the self-styled 'Strathspey King', in 'the handsome Highland dress with scarlet waistcoat and fine lace jabot that [he] wore on the concert platform'. Possessed of great energy, as well as of a healthy 'guid conceit' of himself, he remarked at the age of eighty-one (three years before his death) that he felt no more than thirty. GRD
Scottish National Portrait Gallery

THE NINETEENTH CENTURY

A combination of favourable circumstances contributed to the prominent place taken by 'Scottish' jewellery in the nineteenth century, more prominent than at at any other period in its long history. Attention was focused on the Celtic heritage by the cycle of taste in art and fashion, but more importantly by royal favour. The importance of George IV's visit to Edinburgh has already been remarked upon.

The part taken by Sir Walter Scott, who stage-managed the royal visit, befitted the man who had already done so much to give Scotland an important role in the Romantic Movement and to promote the sense of national identity that is an important feature of nineteenth-century historicism. In 1815 he had proposed to the then Prince Regent that a commission should be set up to examine the Crown Room at Edinburgh Castle, and in 1817 the lost regalia, the 'Honours of Scotland', were disinterred under the supervision of the Commissioners. In the following year the public were admitted to view the jewels in a treasury at Edinburgh Castle.

Meanwhile the novels that were to make Scott one of the most successful and celebrated authors of the century were appearing in rapid succession, giving a Scottish dimension to the Romantic historical revival. The *Ivanhoe* Ball which took place in 1823 was one of the fancy dress entertainments that played an important part in popularising revivalist styles. The costumes at the Eglinton Tournament, banquet and ball, which was held at Eglinton Castle in Ayrshire in 1839, also provided models which filtered in a modified form into contemporary dress.

Mary, Queen of Scots was an appropriately tragic focus for the Romantic Movement in Scotland, manifested in the popularity of the silver crowned double-heart brooches that were taken as emblems forming an 'M' for Mary (29). The silver Memento Mori watch in the form of a skull, supposed to have belonged to Mary, was lent to the 1889 *Royal House of Stuart* exhibition in London by a descendant of Walter Scott's friend, Sir Thomas Dick Lauder, author and antiquary. Mary was often chosen for fancy dress, for example, by the Princess of Wales for the Waverley Ball held at Marlborough House in 1871.

detail of 55 Countess of Elgin

Striving for accuracy, in date at least, the Marchioness of Lorne (Queen Victoria's daughter, Princess Louise) wore with her Mary, Queen of Scots costume the pendant from a portrait in the Royal Collection of Elizabeth I as a Princess, then attributed to Holbein. This may have been one of many versions made by Robert Phillips of Cockspur Street in London. For their marriage, the Marquess had commissioned from Phillips a tiara of leaves and buds of bog-myrtle, emblem of the Campbell clan. The Marian cult and the subtle relationship between fancy dress and fashion resulted in a taste among Scottish patrons for Tudor or 'Holbeinesque' jewellery. It is significant that the only inscribed enamelled gold 'Holbeinesque' pendant so far recorded should be a memento of Robert Baird of Auchmeddan, 1856.

Indigenous materials played an important part in Scottish revivalism. Scottish firms made a speciality of jewellery set with local hardstones – mainly granite quarried near Perth – using a technique of intarsia or inlay that has its beginnings in Renaissance Italy and had been brought to a peak of technical sophistication in Dresden in the eighteenth century. The German connection is significant, since the popularity of 'Scottish' jewellery outran the capacity of the native lapidaries and much material had to be sent to workshops at Idar-Oberstein for cutting and polishing. The speciality of these workshops was the improvement of colour by staining and heat treatment; probably they were not above some discreet substitution of disappointing material. The metal-working was also contracted out, and many 'Scottish' pieces were made in Birmingham and Newcastle, for example by Lister & Sons of Newcastle-on-Tyne, who exhibited 'Highland ornaments' at the Great Exhibition in 1851.

detail of 61 Susan, Duchess of Hamilton

Many of the hardstone jewels are embellished with cairngorms – or when they ran out, as they quickly did, colour-enhanced citrines – and river pearls from the Tay. Effie and John Ruskin, on their Scottish honeymoon in the spring of 1848, thought of acquiring some pearls and cairngorms from the celebrated Peter McAlpin of Killin but found it was the wrong season. Whole families fished for pearls at the height of the demand in the 1860s – in 1867 the *Englishwoman's Domestic Magazine* remarked, 'Scotch jewellery as well as Scotch costume is *de rigueur*' – and the river banks were piled with rotting heaps of mussel-shells.

The importance of Queen Victoria's attachment to Scotland in promoting this enthusiasm for Scottish ornaments can hardly be over-stressed. When they were at Balmoral the family dressed in 'Highland things' and the Queen delighted in giving and receiving Scottish jewellery. She gave Lady Augusta Stanley a kilt-pin for her small son, the future Dean of Windsor.

Queen Victoria was not elegant nor were her *toilettes* well matched, the jewellery often in garish competition with the colours of her dress. However, when she and Albert visited Napoleon III and the Empress Eugenie in Paris in 1855, her tartans and the Highland costumes of their children provoked admiration and emulation, not only in textiles but also in enamelled gold, Auguste Lion producing a *chain écossais*.

CHARLOTTE GERE

55 Mary Nisbet, Countess of Elgin, by François-Paul-Pascal Simon, Baron Gérard, about 1803.

Mary Nisbet was the only daughter of William Hamilton Nisbet. She married Thomas Bruce, 7th Earl of Elgin in 1799 and accompanied him on his diplomatic mission to the Porte. He was responsible for the transfer from Athens to London of the Parthenon sculptures, the 'Elgin Marbles', acquired by the British government in 1816. Following the breakdown of the Peace of Amiens in 1803 the Elgins were detained in France, and on 24 November Lord Elgin was arrested in retaliation for the capture and imprisonment of General Boyer in the West Indies. It was probably at this time that the portrait was painted by the celebrated Baron Gérard, favourite artist of the Bonapartes: his picture of the Emperor's mother of this same date is a recent addition to the National Gallery collection in Edinburgh. The necklace worn by Lady Elgin is most unusual. From the upper gold chain depend ancient coins, anticipating the mid-nineteenth-century interest in archaeological pieces. The coins are explained by Lord Elgin's interest in antiquities. Coin-set jewellery has a long history, enjoying periods of popularity in Roman jewellery from the third century AD and surfacing again in the Byzantine period, when the coin-set ornament had a specific or symbolic association with marriage. Such antiquarianism would surely have appealed to Lord Elgin. A large, faceted green stone in a neo-Gothic setting is suspended from the lower chain, and if this pendant dates from their marriage four years earlier, Lady Elgin would have been in advance of fashion in choosing a neo-Gothic setting, popular enthusiasm for which followed the first experiments with cast-iron work in Berlin in 1804.

In 1808 Lord and Lady Elgin were divorced, after which she married Robert Ferguson of Raith and he married Elizabeth Oswald of Dunnikier. Following the death of her second husband, Lady Elgin spent most of her time at Archerfield, Dirleton in East Lothian. CG
National Gallery of Scotland

Edinburgh typist who died in 1990, bequeathing a huge collection of costume jewellery and other decorative items to the National Museums of Scotland. She also left diaries which detailed every item of her income and expenditure for some forty years.

The chain was given to the National Museums of Scotland by an acquaintance, to whom Miss Crowford had written: 'Regrettably, I don't know the Christian name of the wearer of the straw (?) chain...She was Mrs ? Crowford, my dear Father's widowed paternal grandmother, an Englishwoman from Hoxton, London, and greatly esteemed by my paternal grandmother whom she visited when the latter was widowed at the age of 28 with a young family of four boys, the youngest being my Father, then only six months old. This fine old English lady undertook the long and tedious journey from London to Berwickshire although poverty-stricken and in failing health. The two items mentioned were left by her as keepsakes on her return south'. Miss Crowford's father was born in 1885.

The weaving of chains and braids out of hair, horsehair or gut was a valued accomplishment and the pieces thus made were usually given as mementos, with, in the case of hairwork, sentimental implications. The mother-of-pearl pendants on the second chain, including a moth, which indicates 'night' or 'death', imply that this piece was also intended as a keepsake or Memento Mori. EG/CG

National Museums of Scotland

56 *Two long chains made up of links of woven thread-fine cat-gut, one with leaf-shaped mother-of-pearl plaques at intervals along its length and a double mother-of-pearl pendant in the form of a moth with an emblematic and inscribed shield-shaped plaque below, mid-nineteenth century.*

The plaque shows two birds, possibly emus, standing on a ground on which is incised a banner with the words FORGET ME NOT, the pendant probably a later addition. The simpler chain, made up of two hundred and twenty oval links of cat-gut, belonged to an ancestor of Miss Eileen Crowford, an

57 *Wilhelmina Campbell, by John Partridge, about 1820.*

This portrait was exhibited at the Royal Academy in 1820. It shows Wilhelmina, daughter of Sir James Colquhoun of Luss and wife of John Campbell, seated, wearing a lace-trimmed satin dress in the height of fashion. She holds a folding case containing her husband's portrait in miniature. Her jewellery consists of a necklace with a pendant in the form of a Maltese cross, a small oval brooch, a pair of bracelets to match the necklace and a wedding ring. Like the dress, her jewellery is in the fashionable taste of the day. A Maltese cross in cornelian and pearls is described and illustrated in the *Belle Assemblée* as early as May 1809, but many survive with sentimental inscriptions dating to the 1820s. Wilhelmina's is of diamonds, as are the matching bracelets. A small oval brooch is pinned to the centre of her neckline. Her wedding ring is very thin, like the other early nineteenth-century gold rings excavated from crypt burials at Christ Church Spitalfields and now in the Museum of London. This may indicate a preference, soon to be supplanted by the much broader bands of the mid-century.   CG

A Private Collection

58 *Gold open-mounted citrine necklace with pendant drop, nineteenth century; Berlin ironwork cross; pair of Berlin ironwork earrings, both first half of the nineteenth century.*

This fine necklace shows the advances that occurred in open-work settings after about 1800. The pavilion, or rear of the stone, was now visible, allowing light to shine through, thereby enhancing the brilliant effect and subtle colours of well-cut stones. Originally produced in the Royal Berlin Factory from 1804, iron jewellery became particularly popular when Prussia rebelled against Napoleon's occupation in 1813. Patriotic women exchanged their gold and jewels for iron jewellery, to help finance the war. The iron jewels were often inscribed 'Gold gab ich fur Eisen, 1813' (I gave gold for iron, 1813). Many of the iron cross pendants date to a few years before this, however, as they were particularly associated with mourning for Queen Luisa of Prussia, who died in 1810. Iron was thought specially appropriate for personal mourning as it signified constancy. The neo-Gothic style decoration which characterised much of this jewellery after the war was also significant, linked as it was to the Prussians' struggle for unification and their idealised notion of a unified Germany in the Middle Ages.

This rather sombre jewellery became popular outside Germany too and remained so until the middle of the nineteenth century. The cross above was bought in 1857 from A Wagenitz, a Berlin jeweller who had exhibited at the Great Exhibition in 1851. A revival of interest occurred during the First World War, when Germans were again asked to part with their gold to help the war effort.   GRD

National Museums of Scotland

59 *Dr Thomas S Traill, by Alexander Mosses, about 1827.*

Masculine jewellery is almost entirely absent from eighteenth-century portraits, but from the 1780s until the 1820s no gentleman with any claim to elegance would have been seen without a bunch of fob seals dangling from his waistcoat. Originally, 'fob' had been the name given to the little trouser pocket, just below the waistband, in which a watch was carried. Later, the term was applied to the chain from which the watch was suspended, and finally it came to refer to the ornaments dangling from the chain.

The wearer in this instance is Dr Thomas Traill the eminent forensic scientist. Born in Orkney, he studied medicine at Edinburgh University and in 1803 moved to Liverpool as a general practitioner. There he and his wife, a Ross-shire girl, brought up their family of five children. He also played an active part in civic life, helping to found the Literary and Philosophical Society of Liverpool. It was during this period that he sat for his portrait to Alexander Mosses, a local drawing master. The picture was exhibited at the Liverpool Academy in 1827. Dr Traill was a man of wide-ranging interests, a life-long lover of the classics and an energetic student of physical geography and meteorology. In 1832 he moved back to Edinburgh to become Professor of Medical Jurisprudence at the University and the following year he was elected a Fellow of the Royal College of Surgeons of Edinburgh. He became its President in 1852.

He was appointed editor of the eighth edition of the *Encyclopaedia Britannica* in 1861, but increasing ill-health prevented him from playing an active role in the project and he died in his Rutland Square house in July 1862, at the age of eighty. RKM
Scottish National Portrait Gallery

60 *Set of fob seals, about 1830.*

These five matched gold fobs are set with white chalcedony, citrine, glass and cornelian intaglios carved with a variety of devices and mottoes. All are recorded in William Tassie's *Catalogue of Mottoes and Devices for Seals etc* of 1830. William was the nephew of James Tassie of Glasgow, the inventor of the glass paste medallions which bear his name. William continued his uncle's business in London, also producing reproductions of ancient and modern engraved gemstones and a huge range of seals. Seals were used from ancient times to make an impression on clay or wax in order to authenticate documents, necessary when literacy was far from general. By the eighteenth century their practical uses were limited and they became mainly a decorative feature of dress. However, both seal fobs and signet rings were used well into the nineteenth century to seal letters and packets with the sender's device or motto. GRD
National Museums of Scotland

61 *Susan Beckford, Duchess of Hamilton, by Willes Maddox, about 1835.*
Susan Euphemia, second and favourite daughter of William Beckford, author and collector, of Fonthill in Wiltshire, in 1810 married Alexander, future 10th Duke of Hamilton, who succeeded to the dukedom in 1819. Susan was imbued with antiquarianism through her upbringing, and she married a man no less ostentatious in his taste, with a love of rich colours and magnificent accessories. It is hardly surprising, therefore, that in her portrait the

Duchess has allowed historicism to dictate her choice of dress and jewellery.
At her forehead she wears a *ferronière*, so called because it is inspired by the ornament worn by Leonardo's *Belle Ferronière*, or Blacksmith's Wife. Her pendant brooch is in the Tudor style, as are the pearl earrings with their long pear-shaped drops. Fashionably wide bracelets are clasped with a profile portrait cameo, probably of shell, and an oblong gold frame containing a miniature. Both clasps may have had compartments for hair in the back. Susan Beckford followed the almost universal practice of the period in cherishing locks of hair from those closest to her. A paper containing a lock of her father's hair, inscribed 'Precious Hair cut off on the fatal 2nd May at Bath, 1844', was preserved in the Hamilton collection. Her dress is obviously mediaeval in inspiration – note particularly the pleated chemise showing at the neckline – though the fashionable cut and shape obscure the antiquarian details. Willes Maddox, the English portraitist and history painter, has depicted the Duchess at the piano. Both her father and the Duke

were passionately fond of music and fortunately she was musically talented. Maddox had been chosen to record objects from Beckford's collection, for the illustrated account of Lansdowne Tower, his last house, as well as producing the two versions of this portrait (the other is at Brodick Castle) and the death-bed portrait of Beckford for his daughter.   CG
Hamilton Collection,
Lennoxlove, East Lothian

62 *Pair of bracelets, faceted garnet-red and steel beads strung in a trellis pattern, box-clasps with gilt stars, early nineteenth century. Bracelet of six composite micro-mosaic plaques, strung with bead spacers, Roman, 1830-40.*
Beadwork, requiring no more than dexterity and patience, was a popular amateur pastime. When produced commercially it was the lowest paid sweated labour, carried out by women in their homes as piecework. Bracelets in pairs were enduringly popular: evidence of their use can be found over more than a century, from delicate examples

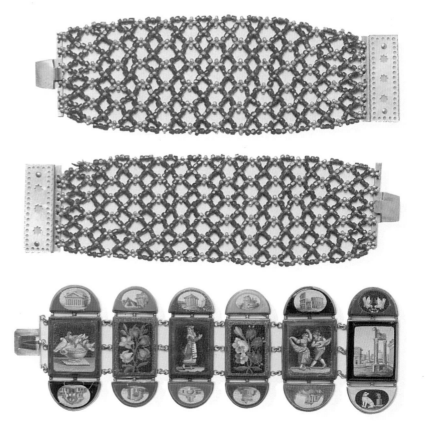

strung with beads and pearls like these and the Atholl bracelets (43) to the heavy wide bands of gold with large clasps worn by the Duchess of Hamilton (61).

The micro-mosaic bracelet is a particularly nice example of this type of admired nineteenth-century Roman souvenir jewellery. The plaques show ten minute ovals of the sites of antiquity as well as a larger view of the Forum. Two of the larger plaques are taken from illustrations of Italian peasant costume, two more are of flowers and two others, one large and one small, show Pliny's doves drinking from the fountain of Venus. The last little oval depicts a seated dog, fidelity, with the butterfly, symbolic of the soul, flying above a votive column, a charming and popular sentimental device. The micro-mosaic pictures are executed in minute glass tesserae [tiles] and inlaid into a plaque of black glass. The flower plaques in this example are bordered with 'adventurine' glass, imitating the gold-flecked stone. The best quality mosaic work is laboriously and lengthily polished to perfect smoothness. CG
National Museums of Scotland

63 Serpent necklace, silver and gold, set with turquoises, pearls, rubies and brilliant-cut diamonds, probably English, about 1835-40.

Since antiquity, the motif of the snake has often been used in jewellery, partly because serpentine coils encircling the wrist or finger form such a pleasing design, partly because of the ancient and beneficent symbolism attached to the creature. Snake rings and bracelets were very popular during the Hellenistic and Roman periods, and many examples have been found at sites such as Pompeii and Herculaneum. During the Victorian era, the motif of the serpent biting its tail was a fashionable symbol of eternity, and was frequently used for both mourning jewels and tokens of love.

The serpent motif was at its most fashionable in the 1840s, although it remained popular throughout the century. Queen Victoria wore a serpent bracelet at her first council meeting in 1837, and her betrothal ring was a gold serpent set with emeralds. As a necklace or bracelet, the snake could be represented in various ways. The body was often made from flexible links resembling scales, set with pavé-set [close set] turquoises, with a ruby for the eye. In sentimental jewellery of the Victorian period, gemstones were carefully chosen for their significance: the ruby denoted exalted love, whilst turquoise had the power to protect its wearer from danger. EG
Victoria and Albert Museum

64 Anne Gordon and her son Robert, attributed to Sir Francis Grant, about 1857.
Anne, wife of Henry Wolrige Gordon, is portrayed holding her eldest son, Sir Robert Gordon Gilmour of Liberton, who was born in 1857. The portrait must date from the first year of the child's life. The blue bows ornamenting Anne's dress are a striking note in the all-white clothes of both mother and baby, and they emphasise the turquoises on the serpent necklace and the interlacing enamel through the links of the bracelet. The sitter is wearing a ring of a half-hoop of turquoises as a keeper to her wedding ring. It may have been her betrothal ring. However, such rings, or eternity rings with stones set right round the hoop, were traditionally given to mark the birth of a child, appropriate in a portrait of a mother with her baby.

Sir Francis Grant, to whom the picture is attributed, was the son of the laird of Kilgraston, in Perthshire. After a long and prolific career, he became President of the Royal Academy, London, in 1866 and was knighted. He died in 1878. CG
Captain Wolrige Gordon of Esslemont

65 *Selection of 'Scotch Pebble' jewellery, mid to late nineteenth century.*

Scotland has numerous rich sources of the fine agates, jaspers, bloodstones, cairngorms and granites which were cut, polished and set in brooches, bracelets, pendants and necklaces. Somewhat misleadingly called 'Scotch Pebbles', they grew in popularity in the mid-nineteenth century, fostered by Queen Victoria's love of Balmoral and the Scottish countryside. She was particularly interested in cairngorms, and her Journal records that she found some on a climb to the top of Beinn a' Bhuird.

Large numbers of lapidaries set up in business, especially in Edinburgh, drawing for their inspiration on recently discovered archaeological treasures, such as the magnificent Hunterston Brooch.

Agates and other semi-precious stones also occur in different parts of the world, and Scottish craftsmen were not alone in producing 'Scotch Pebble' jewellery. At the Great Exhibition of 1851, work from London, Exeter and Germany was exhibited. Scottish forms were also copied by workers in Birmingham, using either Scottish stones or local materials. The most popular designs were frequently registered at the Patent Office. This makes it possible to discover their origins: otherwise it is extremely difficult to tell where particular pieces were made.

The popularity of this distinctive and colourful jewellery declined just before the Great War, and the last true Edinburgh-based lapidary, Alexander Begbie, died in 1958 aged eighty-three. GRD
National Museums of Scotland

66 *Lady Agnew of Lochnaw, by John Singer Sargent, about 1892-3.*

Gertrude, younger daughter of the Honourable Gowran Charles Vernon, barrister and recorder of Lincoln and his wife Caroline Fazackerley, married Sir Andrew Noel Agnew, 9th Baronet, barrister-at-law, on 15 October 1889. This portrait, painted about 1892-3, turned the sitter into a society celebrity and confirmed the artist's fame and popularity, a change from the storm of criticism that had greeted his daring portrait of Madame Gautreau, shown at the Paris *Salon* eight years before and the somewhat equivocal reception of his previous Royal Academy exhibits. Sargent's deft impressionistic touches of paint suggest the jewellery rather than delineate it precisely. In this portrait we can only guess at an aquamarine pendant in a setting of turquoise blue flowers. The beautifully painted giltwood bergère and the silk draperies, which so perfectly set off the shimmering white dress with its mauve sash and sleeve bows, were just studio props, but the suggestion of a taste for French eighteenth-century decoration is appropriate to the delicacy of the jewel.

Lady Agnew, who had no children, died on 3 April 1932, seven years after her portrait came to the National Gallery of Scotland. CG
National Gallery of Scotland

67 *Marriage jewel for Lady Bute, designed by William Burges, 1872-3, and the Bute bridesmaid's locket, 1872.*

The enamelled gold brooch set with faceted and cabochon gems and pearls in the form of a Gothic-style capital letter 'G' surmounted by a coronet was supplied by the famous architect William Burges to Gwendolen, Lady Bute more than a year after her marriage had taken place. On the reverse, the bride's married initials, GMAB, appear in the centre of the jewel.

The wedding of John Patrick Crichton-Stuart, 3rd Marquess of Bute to Gwendolen Mary Anne Howard, had been celebrated on 16 April 1872. Burges had completed the design for the brooch only a fortnight earlier and he did not finish the jewel until September 1873. The inspiration for it came from a brooch in the form of a Gothic 'G' in the portrait then believed to be of Katherine Parr but since identified as Lady Jane Grey. Painted by Master John, the picture is now in the National Portrait Gallery in London. The Bute bridesmaids' locket/brooches were ordered in February 1872, in good time for the wedding, from Mackay, Cunningham and Company, Goldsmiths to the Queen, of 62 Princes Street, Edinburgh. The lockets are more conventional than the Gothic 'G' brooch, consisting as they do of an armorial shield in enamelled gold, surmounted by a coronet over a circle set with diamonds and rubies. This type of armorial bridesmaid's jewel was popular in the nineteenth century, examples surviving from ducal and other aristocratic marriages.   CG

A Private Collection

THE TWENTIETH CENTURY

VI

The primary purpose of jewellery is adornment. With the exception of some late twentieth-century work which has the entirely different intention of provoking a reaction in order to make a social statement, it is generally intended to enhance the appearance of its wearer. In all periods, jewellery has been used to convey important messages. These have traditionally been associated with wealth and status but, throughout the twentieth century, messages relating to attitude and lifestyle, and which express a specific personal image, have been equally potent. The jewellery of the Arts and Crafts movement provides one example of this.

In 1873, Christopher Dresser wrote, 'If the work is beautiful then it is ridiculous to estimate its value as though the material of which it is composed were of greater worth than the amount of life, thought, and painstaking care expended upon its production'. Dresser was one of the Victorian designers who greatly influenced the artists of the Craft Revival movement. In 1900, *The Studio* said of the work of the Arts and Crafts jewellers Arthur and Georgie Gaskin (see 77), 'They have developed already a distinctive character for their jewellery, with its stones chosen not for their worth in money but solely on account of their aesthetic value..., wrought entirely by hand, with none of the mechanically accurate symmetry which, however tasteless, is considered essential in the trade'. This emphasis on aesthetics over intrinsic monetary value, and craft skill over mass-production, is a theme which recurs frequently in the story of twentieth-century jewellery.

In Scotland, there were several important Arts and Crafts artists designing and producing jewellery. The work of the Glasgow School was much admired on the Continent, and influenced many international designers. The Glasgow-trained Macdonald sisters and Jessie M King are perhaps the best-known, but the jewellery of East Coast artists such as Phoebe Traquair (see 74), Lady Gibson Carmichael and James Cromar Watt is also beginning to be appreciated. The inspiration and values of the Craft Revival movement can still be seen in later works by jewellers such as Sibyl Dunlop (see 71).

detail of 76 Flora Drummond

detail of 70 Joan Wolrige Gordon

In the early years of the century, strict rules concerning correct dress were still followed in elegant British society, and precious jewellery was very formal. For those who, for whatever reason, could not wear real gems, there was a flourishing trade in convincing imitations. But there was also a quite different type of ornament, known as dressmaker's jewellery, which was not made using jewellery techniques, and which was both expensive and fashionable (see 69). It was only after the First World War that these two elements fused to become what we now think of as costume jewellery. This type of jewellery was appreciated for its decorative qualities; its materials are irrelevant. In a later decade, in a neat reversal of values, Mrs Wallis Simpson excited comment by wearing the real thing as if it were costume jewellery. Mrs Belloc Lowndes wrote of her in 1937, 'She wore a very great deal of jewellery, which I thought must be what is called "dressmaker's jewels", so large were the emeralds in her bracelets and so striking and peculiar a necklace'. Costume jewellery has tended to survive in greater quantity than fashionable precious jewellery, precisely because it was made from non-precious materials: it was less likely to be broken up and re-worked. However, at the present time, far less has been written about it.

The First World War and the Russian Revolution saw much precious jewellery disappear. When the war ended, society re-emerged with changed attitudes and values. Paris was the centre of fashion and taste. This may be partly because the artistic community and the upper echelons of society mixed so freely there. The 1920s and 1930s were dominated by the Art Deco style. Named after the great Paris exhibition of *Arts Décoratifs et Industriels Modernes* in 1925, the roots of the style were actually pre-war. The influence of couturiers, designers and artists on jewellery design was especially notable. Chanel and Verdura, Schiaparelli and Schlumberger made exciting partners.

Another important factor which affected post-war jewellery design was the changed role of women. Newly-emancipated, less constrained in their tastes and activities, they demanded and wore a quite different type of jewellery.

The 1920s and 1930s were decades of experimentation with new, non-precious materials. For high fashion wear, different kinds of plastics, such as bakelite, celluloid and the 1930s discovery, acrylic, could be used to create light and brilliantly-coloured ornaments. Metals such as chrome and steel reflected an interest in machinery, and were used for jewels in a modernistic style.

The Second World War and post-war austerity, not surprisingly, exerted a depressing influence on jewellery design in Britain. There was little work which represented much advance on designs of the previous decade. The 1950s saw the beginnings of re-generation. The major source of inspiration was Scandinavian design, with its strong, clean lines and simple unadorned surfaces. The talented designers employed by the firm of Jensen were particularly important. The young jewellers of the 1960s drew their inspiration from nature, producing 'organic' jewels, often based on found objects and uncut stones. The spirit of the decade enabled a new freedom to experiment, to dispense with convention, which has characterised late twentieth-century work.

In the final years of the century, jewellers continue to experiment with new techniques in traditionally precious materials, as well as new materials. Jewellery today tends to fall into distinct categories: precious, rather more traditional limited-production work, retailed by expensive specialist jewellers; mass-produced fashion jewellery and lower-cost precious metal items, retailed by high street jewellers and department stores; and unique pieces made by designer-jewellers, retailed at galleries and exhibitions. There is relatively little overlap, although the public is beginning to discover that original handmade designer pieces may be as inexpensive as chainstore jewellery.

Many different types of jewellery are being made in Scotland. Traditional Scottish designs, such as luckenbooth brooches and 'Scotch Pebble' jewellery, are still produced for both the home and the tourist market. Several very successful commercial firms also produce jewellery inspired by motifs evocative of the nation's ancient and historical past, re-worked to please today's customers, and sold widely outside Scotland; and Scotland is home to many talented and original designer-jewellers. They use both traditional and newer materials, and their work makes an important contribution to British contemporary jewellery as a whole. Scots in the late twentieth century wear all these kinds of jewellery – but also closely follow international styles and fashions.

Few of the recent developments can be traced through portrait painting. As the century progressed, people have turned increasingly to photographic portraiture, and even amongst the moneyed and aristocratic classes, it became fashionable to have a portrait taken by one of the best society photographers. Portrait painting seems to be reserved for particular occasions. Perhaps as a result of its more formal nature, sitters tend to choose their most important jewels, often family pieces, usually antique, for the image they wish to convey for posterity (70). It is rare for painted portraits to show major contemporary or high-fashion jewellery.

In the second half of the century, the barriers are breaking down between jewellery and art. People are less likely to question the value of an article of jewellery based only on the cost of the materials used to make it. Artists like Peter Chang, with his meticulous, time-consuming work in an intrinsically worthless medium (81), represent those creating wearable art. The art of jewellery is today not simply the art of portraying jewellery, the art of making it or the art of wearing it; jewellery has become art.

ELIZABETH GORING

81 Peter Chang brooch

68 *Mabell Gore, Countess of Airlie, by Sir Oswald Birley, 1930.*

Lady Mabell Frances Elizabeth Gore, daughter of the 5th Earl of Arran, married David, 11th Earl of Airlie in 1886. They had three sons and three daughters. When the Earl was killed in action in the Boer War, Lady Airlie was immediately approached by the Princess of Wales (later Queen Mary) to be one of her ladies-in-waiting. She declined because of her young family, but the Princess put forward the claims of childhood friendship and she was prevailed upon to change her mind. For more than fifty years she remained as beloved friend and confidante.

As a peeress, Lady Airlie had the title of Lady of the Bedchamber. She shared with her royal mistress a dignified way of dressing designed to please King George V. In her memoirs she remarked of Queen Mary, 'She never even wore a colour which the King did not like. Her style of dressing was dictated by his conservative prejudices; she was much more interested in fashion than most people imagined, and sometimes I think longed in secret to get away from the hats and dresses which were always associated with her'.

No longing, however intense, would have made the Queen oppose his wishes and her style in dress and jewellery took on a timeless and reassuring dignity. From the 1920s, Lady Airlie wore the combination of four-strand pearl choker and long ropes of pearls shown in Sir Oswald Birley's portrait, no doubt maintaining the view current when she was a young woman, that no jewellery can be more flattering or magnificent than a profusion of the finest pearls. CG

A Private Collection

69 *Long necklace, glass pastes and imitation pearls on a silk and cotton band, unknown maker, about 1918.*

This necklace was given to the former Royal Scottish Museum in 1970 by the Lady Victoria Wemyss of Wemyss Castle, Fife. Lady Victoria, a former Woman of the Bedchamber to HM Queen Elizabeth the Queen Mother, is the daughter of the 6th Duke of Portland. Queen Victoria, after whom she was named, stood sponsor for her in person. In 1991, Lady Victoria celebrated her one hundred and first birthday. She recalled that she had been given the necklace on the occasion of her wedding to Captain Michael John Erskine Wemyss on 25 November 1918.

It consists of a carpet of paste gems mounted on individual metal mounts stitched to a flexible silk and cotton band. The pastes are of excellent quality: this is costume jewellery at its best, both expensive and fashionable. It was probably made by outworkers for a high-class dressmaker. Similar necklaces might have been purchased by the kind of wealthy, artistic clientèle who patronised firms such as Liberty and Company.

The Victoria and Albert Museum have three long glass and clay bead necklaces made by Winifred Gill for the Omega Workshops around 1916. Winifred Gill, once secretary to Joan Fry, was employed by the Workshops from 1913 to 16. She bought brightly coloured beads from Woolworths, and strung them whilst travelling on a train from Guildford to the Omega with Roger Fry. They appealed to him ('Just like a Picasso', he said), and the Omega started to sell similar necklaces.

At this period costume jewellery was extremely popular and indeed, if it was not real, then it had to be obviously fake. Pastes were no longer simply imitations but fashionable accessories. It is Coco Chanel who is generally credited with making artificial jewellery acceptable for day wear, declaring, 'It does not matter if they are real, so long as they look like junk'. Her jewels, and jewellery of this quality, were recognised for their decorative worth. EG

National Museums of Scotland

70 *Joan Wolrige Gordon, by John M Hay, about 1928.*

Joan Walter married the Aberdeenshire landowner, Captain Robert Wolrige Gordon MC of Hallhead and Esslemont in 1927. She was a grand-daughter of the Macleod of Macleod and in the absence of a Macleod successor, her second son John became the 29th Chief of Macleod in 1976.

In this portrait she wears a chemise dress of black silk shot with silver, a stole of sea-green silk having fallen from her shoulders. Her pendant, the Hallhead Cross, of rose diamonds in a plain silver mount, was brought back from France by Robert Gordon, 11th of Hallhead, before he bought Esslemont in 1728. She had worn it at her wedding, as do all the brides marrying the Esslemont heir. Her emerald bracelet was brought into the family by Lady Agnes Northcote, her paternal grandmother.

The Aberdeen artist John A M Hay painted Captain Wolrige Gordon in 1928, and this portrait of his wife, which is of the same dimensions, is evidently a companion piece. Hay lived for many years in London, exhibiting regularly at the Royal Society of Portrait Painters. He finally moved to Oxford and died in 1960. CG

Captain Wolrige Gordon of Esslemont

71 *Pendant cross, silver, garnets and silk,*
by Sibyl Dunlop, about 1925; pendant
necklace, silver, rock crystal, moonstones,
coral and pearls, by Henry George Murphy,
1920s.

Sibyl Dunlop was one of only a small
number of women who became well-known
as jewellers in the early part of the twentieth
century. She was born to Scottish parents in
about 1889. At the turn of the century she
was sent to Brussels to study French, and it
was here that she learned to make jewellery.
In the early 1920s she opened a shop, with
its own workshop, in Kensington Church
Street, London. The books were kept by her
old nurse, Nanny Frost, who lived upstairs.
The workshop was run by W Nathanson
who joined her, aged sixteen, straight from
art school. Her four craftsmen all worked in
full view of the customers. Stones were
specially cut for her by lapidaries in Idar-
Oberstein in Germany. The firm closed in
1939 for the duration of the war, Nathanson
working as a fireman throughout the Blitz.
Sibyl's health deteriorated and she was
unable to continue with her jewellery when
Nathanson re-opened the shop at the end of
the war. She died in 1968 and Nathanson
retired three years later.

Sibyl Dunlop's style was rooted in the
traditions of the Craft Revival movement.
Her output represents some of the best of
late Arts and Crafts work, which by the
1920s and 1930s had become rather an
anachronism. Her designs found their
inspiration in nature, and stylised leaves and
beadwork, as on this pendant cross, are
typical elements of her style. The cross,
which dates from about 1925, is set with
nine almandine garnets. The remarkable
central stone has a hollowed-out back and
carved concentric rows of petals on the
front. The cross is suspended from a cord of
braided red, pink and white silk strands,
with a small silver slider.

Henry George Murphy was born in 1884.
When he was twelve, he was employed by
the great Arts and Crafts jeweller Henry
Wilson to run errands at sixpence a time.
Wilson noticed his genuine interest in
jewellery-making and encouraged him to try

it for himself. Murphy's natural talent led
him from errand boy to assistant, and by
1909 he was teaching alongside Wilson at
the Royal College of Art. In 1912 he went to
Berlin to work with another prominent
goldsmith, Emil Lettré, and the following
year set up his own workshop in London.
He became Principal of the Central School
two years before his death in 1939.

Like Sibyl Dunlop, Murphy's work was
based in the Arts and Crafts tradition.
However, his later jewellery was influenced
by contemporary trends in France. The
Ballets Russes, led by Diaghilev, with designs
by Bakst, provided a particular source of
inspiration, which is reflected in this pendant
necklace. EG

National Museums of Scotland

72 *Mabel Anson, Lady Forbes, by E F Wells, 1925.*

Lady Mabel Anson, second daughter of the 3rd Earl of Lichfield, married Atholl, 21st Baron Forbes in 1914. They had two sons, one of whom died in infancy; the elder succeeded as the present Lord Forbes in 1953. Lady Forbes was portrayed in 1925, wearing a gold and pink patterned woven silk tissue dress with a fur-trimmed velvet evening cloak falling from her shoulders. The long, many-stranded seed-pearl necklace caught at intervals with four oblong diamond clasps set in an openwork pattern was a favourite piece of jewellery given to her by her parents. It is complemented by pearl drop earrings, a most elegant and highly fashionable ensemble. The terms used for jewellery in the early part of the present century – *sautoir*, negligée, rope, bandeau – show the connection with fabrics and ribbons. These are 'dress-maker' jewels that perfectly complete the deceptively simple lines of fashionable costume at this date, though the finest gem-set examples transcend such categorisation.   CG

A Private Collection

73 Two sautoirs, *glass beadwork and silk, 1900-1920; long necklace, glass beads and pastes, 1920s.*

Fine glass beads for the beadwork popular in the nineteenth century were imported from Venice and Bohemia and were expensive, but cheaper British and French beads were also available from haberdashers and pedlars. They were sold by weight, or bought threaded on cotton in bunches. An American commercial machine, the Cornely, invented in 1865, was adapted at the end of the nineteenth century so that it could attach thousands of tiny beads to clothing and accessories. It was widely used in the 1920s, and is still employed today.

In 1903, Herbert Austin, of Boston, Massachusetts, patented the Apache Bead Loom, a frame for weaving beadwork belts, chains, purses and other accessories, which could be used at home. It could produce panels of beadwork patterns, linked by separate strings of beads to form bracelets or necklaces. The designs were often influenced by textiles. The National Museums of Scotland have an example of 'Allen's Improved Bead-Work Loom' which was supplied to a Mrs Green, staying at the

Imperial Hotel, Russell Square, London by John Allen (Bead Importer) of Regent Street and Oxford Street, London. Simpler looms could be made at home from old cigar boxes. Beadwork jewellery and costume accessories could also be purchased at haberdashery shops.

Sautoirs were very fashionable in the first part of the twentieth century. The most expensive were long ribbons of woven seed pearls or diamonds with fringed tassels at either end. They were worn doubled or trebled around the neck, tucked into the skirt or looped over the bodice. Cheaper versions were also popular. Long necklaces of strings of beads, caught at intervals by large bead spacers, were very popular in the

1920s. They could be made from precious materials such as diamonds, pearls, coral and semi-precious stones, but non-precious versions were widely available. The colours and the length were all-important, and the necklaces were the ideal accessory for the flapper dress. EG

National Museums of Scotland

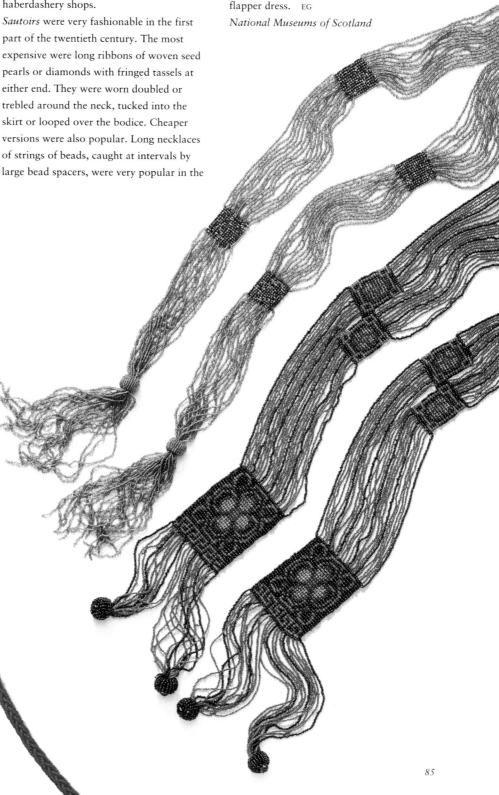

74 *Phoebe Traquair, self-portrait, 1911.*
Phoebe Anna Traquair was the most
important Arts and Crafts artist in the East
of Scotland. She was particularly versatile,
producing fine work in a multiplicity of
media. Her output includes illuminated
manuscripts, murals, paintings,
bookbindings, embroideries, metalwork and
enamelling. She was a prominent member of
the Edinburgh Arts and Crafts Club.
Phoebe was born in Dublin and studied at
the Dublin School of Art. According to an
article in *The Studio* in 1905, she 'betrayed

no special artistic capacity until one day,
after a visit to an exhibition in Dublin, she
became possessed by a desire to paint'. In
1872 she married Ramsay Traquair, who
became Keeper of Natural History at the
Edinburgh Museum of Science and Art (later
to become the Royal Scottish Museum), and
settled in Edinburgh. According to *The
Studio*, she did not fully develop her talent
as an artist for another thirteen or fourteen
years, 'her children being then past the age
when they required constant care'.
This self-portrait, executed at the age of
fifty-nine, is somewhat austere. She is
wearing an artist's smock, in which she is
also depicted in one of her rare published
portraits, a photograph which appeared in
the catalogue of the second exhibition of the
Guild of Women Binders, 1898-9. Jewellery
is notably absent from both portraits.   EG
Scottish National Portrait Gallery

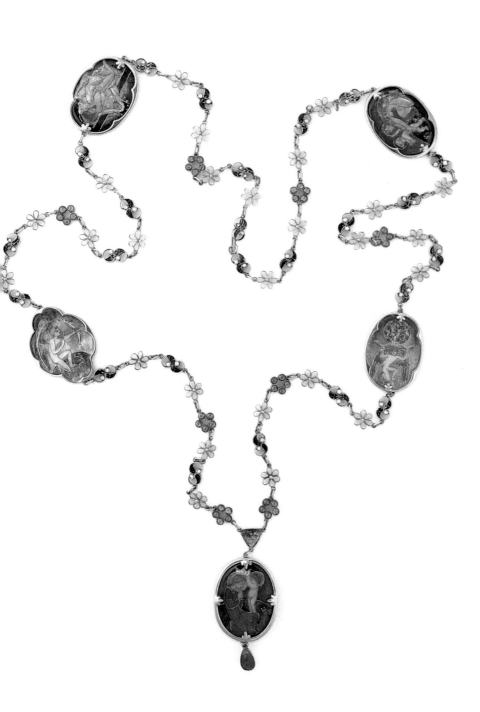

75 *Necklace, gold and enamel, the central pendant titled 'The Earth Upholder Cupid', enamels signed and dated 1895 and 1905; necklace, gold and enamel, with double-sided enamel plaques, some dated 1917 and 1918; both by Phoebe Traquair.*

Phoebe Traquair's enamels were strongly influenced by the work of Sir Edward Burne-Jones and the Pre-Raphaelites. She frequently used allegorical, spiritual or religious subjects. 'The Earth Upholder Cupid', which appears in different versions on both these necklaces, seems a particular favourite. A pendant dated 1902 and a necklace dated 1908, both sharing this same subject, are in the Victoria and Albert Museum.

Enamelling, which experienced a revival of interest around 1900, was one of the most important aspects of Arts and Crafts jewellery. The principles of the movement were based on those of medieval workshops, where the craftsman could design, develop and execute his own work from beginning to end, and where there was little room for specialisation. However, few Arts and Crafts jewellers could achieve a high standard in all areas of the work. Enamelling, although posing particular technical difficulties, was one aspect which could not be surpassed for quality in commercial workshops. It became a favourite pastime amongst the middle and upper classes. Although the standard of Arts and Crafts enamels is variable, some highly skilled jewellers emerged.

The best and most important was Alexander Fisher, who greatly influenced the work of Phoebe Traquair. He used fragments of metal foil in his enamels, which heightens the colours, and this technique is visible in Phoebe's work as well. According to *The Studio*, Phoebe was shown the rudiments of enamelling by Lady Carmichael, who had learned from Fisher. 'Straightway she ordered a stove, set to work, and, as soon as her experience warranted it, launched into such ambitious objects as a triptych, containing thirteen enamels'. EG
National Museums of Scotland

the winter. Although she passed all the qualifying examinations, she was barred from a career as a postmistress – the highest position then available to women in the civil service – by new height regulations. She was an inch shorter than the minimum 5'2".

She moved to London in 1906 to become actively involved with Mrs Pankhurst and the Women's Social and Political Union, leading a systematic campaign of disruption on behalf of the suffragette movement. This resulted in nine terms of imprisonment and five hunger-strikes. One of her proudest possessions was her silver suffragette badge, presented to those who had served a prison sentence, with a bar signifying she had been force-fed.

Flora Drummond became 'General Officer of Field Forces', a role she discharged in full uniform, complete with epaulettes and cap. She was one of the few working-class leaders of the movement. In 1908 she danced the Highland Fling outside Holloway Prison on the release of a Scottish suffragette, and the following year led a massive demonstration in Edinburgh. When war was declared she worked to persuade the government to employ women in industry and in 1920 she founded the Women's Guild of Empire to campaign for equality of opportunity and pay. Flora married twice, first a journeyman upholsterer, then a marine engineer, killed by a V1 flying bomb during the Second World War. She named her one son Keir Hardie Drummond. She died in Argyll, aged seventy, in 1949.

This portrait was commissioned by suffragettes, and hung in the Forum Club, one of the first women's clubs. She proudly wears her medal with a ribbon in the suffragette colours of green, white and violet (signifying Give Women the Vote), and an important necklace, in Arts and Crafts style, set with purple, green and blue stones. The designer and current whereabouts of the necklace remain unknown, but some of Flora's medals were recently given to the Arran Heritage Museum, Brodick, by her daughter-in-law.   EG

Scottish National Portrait Gallery

76 *Flora Drummond, by Flora Lion, 1936.* The remarkable Flora Drummond, suffragette 'General', was born in Manchester although Scottish by descent. She worked as a girl telegraphist on the island of Arran in the summer, studying at the Civil Service College in Glasgow during

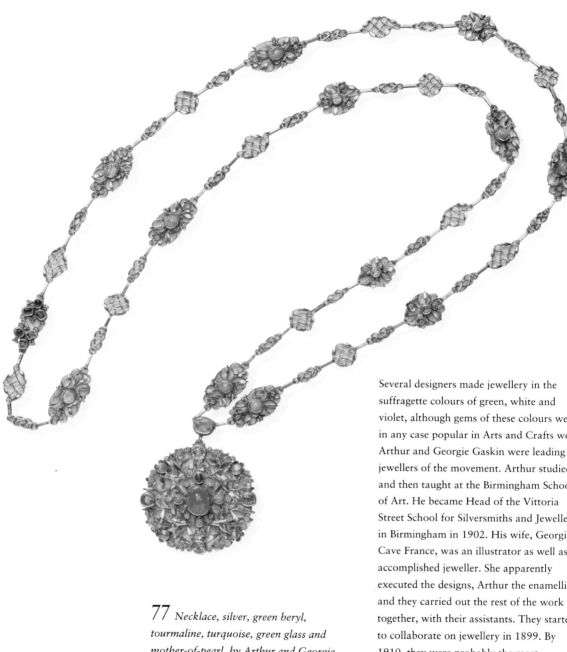

*77 Necklace, silver, green beryl,
tourmaline, turquoise, green glass and
mother-of-pearl, by Arthur and Georgie
Gaskin, about 1910.*

Emmeline Pankhurst, the suffragette leader,
was a supporter of the Arts and Crafts
movement, and once worked in a shop
which sold Arts and Crafts jewellery. Her
daughter, Christabel, is portrayed in both a
photograph (in the Fawcett Library) and a
watercolour (in the Museum of London)
wearing jewellery by C R Ashbee, founder of
the Guild of Handicraft. Ashbee had no
direct link with the suffragette movement,
but his wife Janet was a sympathiser who
corresponded with Christabel Pankhurst.

Several designers made jewellery in the
suffragette colours of green, white and
violet, although gems of these colours were
in any case popular in Arts and Crafts work.
Arthur and Georgie Gaskin were leading
jewellers of the movement. Arthur studied
and then taught at the Birmingham School
of Art. He became Head of the Vittoria
Street School for Silversmiths and Jewellers
in Birmingham in 1902. His wife, Georgie
Cave France, was an illustrator as well as an
accomplished jeweller. She apparently
executed the designs, Arthur the enamelling,
and they carried out the rest of the work
together, with their assistants. They started
to collaborate on jewellery in 1899. By
1910, they were probably the most
influential of the Arts and Crafts jewellers,
and Arthur, who remained Head of the
Vittoria Street School into the 1920s,
inspired generations of students. Liberty &
Company made designs influenced by their
work, although it was not readily adaptable
to mass-production.

The pendant and several elements of the chain
are signed with a G on the back. A necklace
in the Victoria and Albert Museum, made by
Georgie Gaskin in around 1920, is ornamented
with similar birds and rosettes.   EG
National Museums of Scotland

78 *Mrs Eleanor Dalyell of the Binns, by Stanley Cursiter, 1945.*

Eleanor Dalyell, only daughter of Sir James Dalyell, 9th Baronet, married Lt Colonel Gordon Loch, who then took the name and arms of Dalyell. The original baronetcy had been granted to Thomas, son of General 'Muscovy Tam' Dalyell in 1685, with the provision that it could descend through 'heirs of tailzie', that is, in the female line.

In 1945 Stanley Cursiter portrayed Mrs Dalyell in a creamy pink satin court dress against misty grey draperies, a subtle scheme well suited to his luxuriously painterly 'Scottish colourist' style. From her shoulder falls a train or shawl of Brussels lace. She is holding an ostrich-feather fan and full-length white kid gloves, which were still *de rigueur* with formal evening dress. As her husband was Unicorn Pursuivant at the Court of the Lord Lyon, she was frequently involved with Court ceremonial.

Cursiter has used a certain amount of artistic licence in depicting the magnificent set of topaz jewellery worn by Mrs Dalyell (79). These were important family heirlooms, passed down from a favourite aunt, and were appropriate accessories for such a formal portrait. Mrs Dalyell did not, however, wear them regularly, preferring simpler and lighter jewellery. She is seen with only part of the suite, dispensing altogether with an elaborate tiara, and one of the pair of matching bracelets has had the central choker link added to it and pinned at her shoulder. With the drape of her shawl this in some ways recalls the use of a plaid brooch in Highland costume.

Mrs Dalyell died in 1972, having granted the historic house of The Binns in West Lothian to the National Trust for Scotland 'for the benefit and enjoyment of the Nation'. CG/GRD

National Trust for Scotland, The Binns

79 Parure of necklace with a girandole pendant/brooch, earrings and a pair of bracelets, of coloured gold chased in the form of wreaths of flowers and leaves, set with large oval topazes, French, about 1840-50.

The superb suite shown here was worn in Cursiter's portrait of Eleanor Dalyell (78), which in some ways conceals its full interest and complexity. The complete parure, which also includes a tiara set with over sixty topazes, can be worn in a variety of ways. The two matched bracelets, now slightly altered from the original, can be joined together by means of a large central topaz-set link and two gold spring-clip links to form a striking choker. The necklace pendant is detachable and can be worn separately as a brooch, and the final drops of the earrings are also detachable.

This remarkable ensemble belonged to Maria Odette Sampayo, daughter of Anthony Teixiera Sampayo of Peterborough House, Fulham and sister of Anthony Sampayo, Minister of France in Hesse. She was a member of a Portuguese Jewish family which originally came from Braganza in northern Portugal. They may have had some connections with Brazil, a possible source for the topazes.

In 1820 Maria married Admiral Sir William Dalyell, 7th Baronet. She probably first met him while he was the Governor of the Naval Hospital in Greenwich, and it was there that they set up home before coming north, first to Charlotte Square, Edinburgh and then to The Binns. A hero of the Napoleonic Wars, where he was once retrieved from the Dead Cart after receiving terrifying wounds in a skirmish off the French coast, Sir William was thought to have been one of the inspirations for C S Forester's Captain Hornblower.

Small, dark and pretty, Maria was a favourite aunt in the large Dalyell family. She was specially fond of the Sea Room in The Binns, with its views of the Forth and its ships, although she always had to keep huge fires burning in it, for she felt the cold keenly. Sir William and she had two sons and two daughters, the youngest of whom, Elizabeth, was still alive when Eleanor Dalyell was growing up at The Binns. Maria died six years after her husband, in 1871.   GRD
A Private Collection

80 *Her Majesty Queen Elizabeth The Queen Mother, by Avigdor Arikha, 1983.*
Pearls, those most flattering of jewels, have been worn and admired throughout the twentieth century. It is well-known that the Queen Mother loves to wear them, and they are the gems which are most closely associated with her, in both public and private life.

In the 1920s, as Lady Elizabeth Bowes Lyon, she wore a long, double string of pearls with a teardrop pearl pendant. The length of the strands reflected the prevailing fashion for long necklaces in the 1920s. In 1923 she was married in pearls, wearing them not only around her neck but also stitched onto the bodice, sleeves and train of her wedding dress.

In the 1930s, when necklaces were worn shorter, she wore her pearls in three strands, which became increasingly shorter during the course of the war. The Queen Mother still wears pearls for choice, at all kinds of events, and the famous three strands have almost become her hallmark.

This portrait, commissioned by the Scottish National Portrait Gallery, was painted in a single day, 6 July 1983, at Clarence House, the Queen Mother's London residence. The artist was born in Bukovina, and spent his youth on a kibbutz near Jerusalem. He now lives and works in Paris. EG
Scottish National Portrait Gallery

81 Bangle, acrylic, polyester resin and mixed materials, 1988: brooch, acrylic and brass, 1989, both by Peter Chang.

Peter Chang's jewellery is made of plastic. 'I wanted something that would reflect the age we live in, and I liked the idea of working with a substance that was throw-away', he said in *Crafts* September/October 1988. This statement is essentially late twentieth-century in concept. It has little to do with traditional values, which expect jewellery to convey signals of wealth and status. Chang's jewellery is very much a product of its time. The 1980s saw changing attitudes towards consumerism and waste, and the work uses only recycled plastic. It is also recognisably art. Chang acknowledges the influence of Miró and Dada.

Peter Chang lives in Glasgow, although he was born and raised in Liverpool. He studied graphics and sculpture at Liverpool College of Art, then went to Paris to study etching. He took a postgraduate diploma in printmaking and sculpture at the Slade. The following thirteen years were spent sculpting in wood and plastic, making furniture and designing for interiors and gardens. He originally made jewellery for his wife, Barbara Santos-Shaw, Head of Printed Textiles at Glasgow School of Art. In 1984 he decided to develop the jewellery further. He has achieved international recognition in this field, and his work has appeared in the fashion collections of Rifat Ozbek as well as the pages of magazines such as *Vogue* and *Harper's Bazaar*.

The bangle incorporates found items such as fragments of coat hangers, felt tip pens, knitting needles and razor blades. It represents forty-three and a half hours of meticulous mosaic work, carried out in the spring of 1988. The brooch is a perfectly-finished maquette, the winning entry in the 'Scottish Gold' competition organised in 1989 by the National Museums of Scotland and the Scottish Gallery, Edinburgh. The body of the brooch simulates Japanese lacquer effects. The crest and eight bosses were intended to be made up from the first gold to be extracted from a newly-discovered source of the metal near Tyndrum. Scotland is rich in the raw materials of jewellery and the art of those who fashion and portray it.   EG

National Museums of Scotland

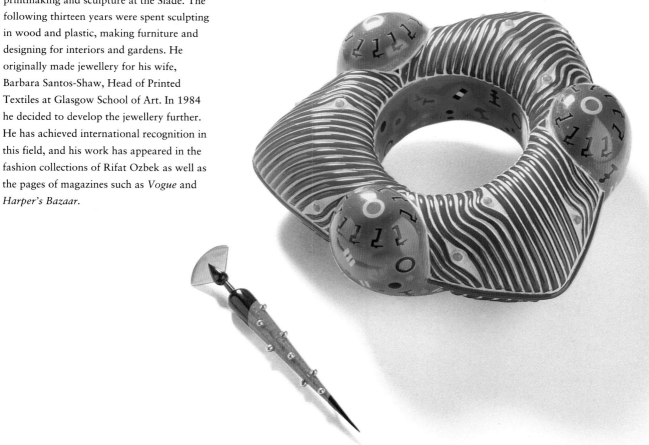

FURTHER READING

Vivienne Becker, *Antique and Twentieth Century Jewellery, A Guide for Collectors* (London 1980)

David Bennett and Daniela Mascetti, *Understanding Jewellery* (London 1989)

Shirley Bury, *An Introduction to Rings* (London 1984)

Barbara Cartlidge, *Twentieth-Century Jewelry* (New York 1985)

Joan Evans, *A History of Jewellery 1100-1870* (London 1953)

Margaret Flowers, *Victorian Jewellery* (London 1951)

Charlotte Gere and Geoffrey C Munn, *Artists' Jewellery: Pre-Raphaelite to Arts and Crafts* (London 1989)

Charlotte Gere, *Victorian Jewellery Design* (London 1972)

Charlotte Gere, *European and American Jewellery 1830-1914* (London 1975)

Guido Gregorietti, *Jewellery through the Ages* (London 1969)

Yvonne Hackenbroch, *Renaissance Jewellery* (London 1979)

Peter Hinks, *Twentieth Century British Jewellery 1900-1980* (London 1983)

Rosalind K Marshall, 'Jewellery in Scottish Portraits 1560-1700' in *The Connoisseur,* April 1978

Rosalind K Marshall, 'The Wearing of Wedding Rings in Scotland' in *Review of Scottish Culture,* ii (Edinburgh 1986)

Daniela Mascetti and Amanda Triossi, *Earrings from Antiquity to the Present* (London 1990)

Harold Newman, *An Illustrated Dictionary of Jewelry* (London 1981)

Charles Oman, *British Rings* (London 1974)

Princely Magnificence: Court Jewels of the Renaissance 1500-1630 ed. Anna Somers Cocks (London 1980)

Diana Scarisbrick, *Ancestral Jewels* (London 1989)

Diana Scarisbrick, *Jewellery in Britain 1066-1837* (London 1991)

Diana Scarisbrick, 'Anne of Denmark's Inventory' in *Archaeologia,* cix (1991)

Hugh Tait, *Catalogue of the Waddesdon Bequest in the British Museum I The Jewels* (London 1986)

Seven Thousand Years of Jewellery ed. Hugh Tait (London 1986)

The Art of the Jeweller: a catalogue of the Hull Grundy Gift to the British Museum, 2 vols ed. Hugh Tait (London 1984)

Lou Taylor, *Mourning Dress* (London 1983)

The Power of Love: Six Centuries of Diamond Betrothal Rings ed. Karen Levi (London 1988)

Treasures and Trinkets: Jewellery in London from pre-Roman Times to the 1930s ed. Tessa Murdoch (London 1991)